Holidazed

A COMEDY

By

Bailly Morse

RIVERSIDE PRESS

Riverside Press
Cummington, MA
authorbaillymorse@gmail.com

ISBN-10: 0-9796233-6-7
ISBN-13: 978-0-9796233-6-3

Holidazed

A COMEDY

By

Bailly Morse

CAST OF CHARACTERS

FRANCINE WALDROOP: (Female, 40s/50s) The kind, sentimental, overly-anxious mother of Alexis and Ben Peters, ex-wife of Carl Peters. Francine is smart but neurotic, and focusses so much on making others happy that sometimes she forgets she deserves love too.

GERTRUDE WALDROOP: (Female, 80s) Francine's sassy, smart, octogenarian mother. She has reverted to teenage-like tendencies and is unlikely to ever act her age. Loves the gentlemen.

ALEXIS PETERS: (Female, 18) Francine and Carl's daughter, Ben's twin. She is independent, as evidenced by her attending a college in Scotland. She loves her mother's eccentricities, but she also wants to strike out on her own and figure out who she really is.

BEN PETERS: (Male, 18) Ben is Alexis' twin, and Francine and Carl's son. He wants to strengthen his relationship with his father, but he is still very close with Francine. He has a creative side he keeps hidden, covering his deeper insecurities with sarcasm and wit.

CARL PETERS: (Male, 50s) Francine's ex-husband and father to Alexis and Ben. He lives in California, where he moved during his mid-life crisis. He is working on being a responsible adult, and is getting better at being in his children's lives thanks to his girlfriend, Shelley.

CAST (Continued)

MICHELLE (SHELLEY) NELSON-OLSON: (Female, late 20s) Second runner-up Miss Minnesota, Shelley is far from a ditz. Perhaps the most insightful and intelligent of the bunch, Shelley is happily paired with the much older Carl Peters. She is hard to dislike.

HANK WILLIAMS: (Male, 40s/50s) Handyman turned tenant Francine, Hank is inadvertently privy to the lives of the Waldroop/Peters family. Fortunately, he doesn't shy away from crazy, and his openness with Francine makes her, for once, feel less anxious.

WALTER WILLIAMS: (Male, 80s) Walter is Hank Williams father, an 80-year-old bad boy who shows up for a few choice lines at the conclusion of the show.

SCENES

Setting: All scenes take place in Francine's kitchen/dining room, in August in New England.

ACT 1

Scene 1: Afternoon
Scene 2: The next morning
Scene 3: "Christmas" morning.
Scene 4: "Birthday New Year" morning.

ACT 2

Scene 1: Morning.
Scene 2: "Halloween Independence Day" dinner.
Scene 3: Later that night.
Scene 4: "Valentine's Day" night.
Scene 5: "Thanksgiving" day.

ACT 1

SCENE 1

Afternoon, Interior. FRANCINE is sitting at the dining table. She
has her sewing machine before her, and is working on something
sparkly and fluffy. It is unclear, but this looks like it could be a
massive dance costume.

FRANCINE is a middle-aged woman. She is the type of woman
who unabashedly wears sweaters for the holidays and
doesn't understand the trend of "ugly sweater par-
ties". Her favorite vacation place is Disney, because
she loves to find magic in the everyday. She likes
white wine with ice cubes, but when it's been a rough
day, she will have a glass or two of red wine. She has
driven a minivan since her children were born. She
doesn't particularly like change, but keeps her smiley
face forward.

As FRANCINE works on the sewing, she is cheerfully tapping
her toes to music coming from her cell phone. When
the landline phone rings, she calls out.

FRAN   Mother? Mom? Can you get that?

There is no answer, the phone rings again.

FRAN   Mom? (She struggles to stop sewing mid-project)
        Moth— oh never mind!

FRAN tries and fails a few times before she stops her music.
Grabs the phone as it lets out the last ring. She presses it to her

ear and walks center downstage.

FRAN   Hello, Peters Household, this is Francine. (Her tone changes from chipper to less-so) Oh, hi, Carl. Yes, ha-ha, I still do answer the phone the same way. Change my name? Back to Francine Waldroop? No, no. I mean, I went to all that trouble to change my name to Peters with the DMV when we got married. Such long lines. Besides, the kids are Peters. So I want to keep the same name as them. Just because you and I are... (Has trouble saying the next word. Whispers it into the phone.) Divorced. I'm whispering because I don't like the word, Carl. (Takes a breath, false cheerfulness) So, why did you call? I know it wasn't to hear the sound of my voice. Right, it wasn't, was it? I mean, of course it wasn't. Silly. (Listens) Calling about Ben? Oh, California. Yes, he seems excited. He will like having you close by while he's at college. I am half tempted to come out there myself, just so I can be nearby him still! Kidding, of course. (She may not have been kidding). Yes, September 5th he flies out. He'll miss orientation, but at least he'll be here for Labor Day. You know, Labor Day. The holiday. Cancel the flight? What are you talking about? What do you mean drive him? Across the whole country, just to pick him up? I mean, I suppose that's a nice gesture. Father-Son time. But no, that's too much to— You want to? Well, I don't know if Ben will want to. You did? And he said yes? Really, he loves the idea of being trapped in a hot car in the middle of summer with you? Well, fine. Sounds like you two decided without me. But yes, as long as he gets there for his first class. I guess you could pick him up the week before. But he will miss Labor Day. Yes, we do things on Labor Day. Sure we do.

As FRANCINE continues to talk, GERTRUDE sticks her head

around the door, stage left. All the audience first sees is an elderly woman, white/gray hair curled, and large glasses. She looks intently at FRANCINE. When she sees she is distracted, she sneaks into the kitchen behind FRANCINE. As she reveals the rest of her body, it is apparent she is not an average old lady. She is wearing skin tight clothing, looking more like a teenager with mesh and leather and pops of color. Despite the appearance of a sexy young thing, she is still wearing comfortable sneakers. GERTRUDE slowly tries to cross the kitchen, avoiding being seen by FRANCINE.

FRANCINE   I'm not going to get into the finer points of Labor Day celebrations with you right now, Carl. Yes, you can pick him up. You can see Alexis too, before she leaves me. She flies out on September 1st. I still don't understand why the kids are both deciding to go so far for school. Scotland, for goodness sake, is across a whole ocean. What do you mean they are escaping? You don't mean me? Ok, because it sounded like that's what you were saying. Once they leave, I'll be here all alone. Well, except for Mom. She's my one comfort. She won't leave me.

At this point, GERTRUDE has reached the outside door and tries to open it, but she knocks over some shoes piled by the door, and FRANCINE turns to see her.

GERT   (Smiling, holding up her hands) Oh, don't mind me, sweetie. Just going out to do some gardening.

FRANCINE   Like heck, Mom. (Into Phone) I gotta go, Carl. Yeah, yeah, I'm sure that day will be fine for you to arrive. Look, I can't talk now. Love you, bye. (Hangs up phone. Moment of realization) Did I just say "love you, bye?"

GERT   You did. Did you forget he's your ex-husband?

FRAN   Oh, God, how embarrassing. He must think I'm still mooning over him.

GERT   He probably doesn't think that.

FRAN   Oh? Why not?

GERT   People accidentally say "love you" all the time hanging up the phone. I once said it to the gynecologist as I walked out of his office. I think he thought I was just happy I didn't have any problems with my lady bits.

FRAN   He's coming here, you know.

GERT   My Gynecologist? Jesus, I thought he retired.

FRAN   No, not Dr. Stirrup. Carl. The father of my children. My Ex-husband.

GERT   Are you going to be alright, sweetie?

FRAN   I don't know yet. He's coming to take Ben away for college. That part I won't like.

GERT   I thought you bought Ben a plane ticket.

FRAN   Carl is going to drive out and pick him up instead.

GERT   (Off topic) Do you think Dr. Stirrup is still alive?

FRAN   He's not single, if you're wondering.

GERT   Oh, please. Do you think Dr. Stirrup always knew he would be a lady doctor?

FRAN   I mean, his name is a bit of a self-fulfilling prophecy.

GERT   If my name was Stirrup I think I'd have been a cowgirl, though. Different kind of stirrup.

FRAN	Well, you're not a Stirrup. You're a Waldroop. Just like I'll be if I change my name back again.
GERT	I hope my name isn't a self-fulfilling prophecy. Anything with droop in the name... (She glances down at her chest, adjusts a push-up bra) There were some droopy qualities about your father.
FRAN	Ugh, Mom, please. (FRAN looks her mother up and down) What are you wearing?
GERT	I got this new getup at the mall during my outing with the girls. It's my new date outfit.
FRAN	There's so much... skin showing.
GERT	Well that's the idea. Barney likes to see a little skin.
FRAN	Oh, so it's Barney now?
GERT	I can see whoever I want to see.
FRAN	Mom, you need to stop sneaking out like this to see men. Last time you took the van you dinged it up. I still haven't been able to afford getting it fixed.
GERT	I'll take public transportation, then.
FRAN	Look, I'm not trying to stop love, Mom. I know you like Barney—
GERT	It's not love, Francie. It's lust. You should see the things a hip replacement can do to reinvigorate a man—
FRAN	That's the last thing I want to see.
GERT	And the leverage he gets with the walker—
FRAN	Ew, enough, Mom. I get it.
GERT	I don't know if you do. It's been a while since you've

felt the touch of a man. The orderly down at the nursing home, Phil, he's a looker. Maybe you should come with, give Phil the once over. He's got big arm muscles. Says he keeps it tight because he has to be ready to restrain unruly residents. A real strapping guy.

FRAN   Unlike you, Mom, I am not ready to start dating again.

GERT   Who said anything about dating?

FRAN   Will you at least put on a coat?

GERT   Don't slut-shame me, Francie.

FRAN   I'm not slut-shaming. I just figured with all that skin and your poor circulation you'd get cold.

GERT   The bus is heated. (Gertrude leaves through the kitchen door in a huff)

FRAN   (Rubbing at her eyes) Can't un-see Barney and his walker.

BEN Enters, walks toward the kitchen.

BEN   You ok, Mom?

FRAN   Oh, of course. There's my handsome boy! (FRAN intercepts BEN and hugs him, kissing him on the forehead)

BEN   (Shrugging her off gently, continuing to kitchen counter and grabbing an apple) I'm not leaving yet, Mom.

FRAN   But you will soon.

BEN   Did Dad call you? I thought I saw his number on caller ID. Though why you still have a landline, I don't know.

FRAN   Your father did call. He told me you talked.

BEN   Yeah, we've been texting. Did he tell you about our road-trip?

FRAN   Yes. I just wish you would have told me that sooner. I have to cancel your flight now.

BEN   Dad figured it would be a good bonding experience, you know? Since Alexis and I haven't seen him much since he moved.

FRAN   Yes. Well, I am sure you will have a great time with him. As long as you get to your classes on time.

BEN   Yeah. Classes. Sounds like they may not start as soon as I thought.

FRAN   Oh, so maybe your father should come get you later?

BEN   No, I still want to be there early. Explore California and stuff.

FRAN   You're going to miss Labor Day.

BEN   Do we celebrate that?

FRAN   I mean, we should. But not usually. I do take solace in the fact that at least you'll be back for all the other holidays this year, though.

BEN   (Uncomfortable) Right. All the other holidays. About that, Mom...

FRAN   What?

BEN   What with travel across the country being so expensive, I don't think I'll be able to come back for... um,

Thanksgiving.

FRAN   What? But Thanksgiving is a huge holiday, Ben. You've never been away for it. What will you eat? Oh goodness, will FedEx allow me to ship you a turkey?

BEN   Well, Dad invited me to spend it with him.

FRAN   Oh. Oh, I see. So he cooks now, does he?

BEN   Actually I think it's his girlfriend who cooks.

FRAN   Girlfriend?!

Suddenly there is a crash outside of the kitchen. FRAN gasps, looks toward the windows.

FRAN   What was that?

GERTRUDE stumbles in through the kitchen door.

GERT   There seems to have been some trouble with the van.

FRAN   The van? You said you were taking the bus.

GERT   The van seems to have backed into the garage door, instead of driving forward.

FRAN   Oh, God. How bad is it?

GERT   It's not that bad.

BEN looks out the window, pulls a face.

BEN   The garage door looks like it's bent around the van.

GERT   The door might be salvageable. (Another crash from outside) Or it might not be. Who can tell, right?

FRAN   Oh for goodness sake. I have to go look at the damage.

FRAN exits to the outside.

BEN   You ok, Grandma?

GERT   Oh yeah. The padding in this bra kept me nice and cushioned when I bumped into the steering wheel. I didn't even feel it.

BEN   (Looking over his Grandmother's clothing) Did you get that outfit at the mall?

GERT   Sure did. It's from that store T&A.

BEN   Do you know what that stands for?

GERT   Textiles and Apparel?

BEN   Tits and Ass.

GERT   Ah. Makes sense, I guess. There were plenty of those on display. But trust me, this was the classiest outfit they had there.

BEN   You couldn't shop at Chadwick's like other grand-mothers, could you?

GERT   Your mother shops at Chadwick's. I don't want to be matchy-matchy.

BEN   She'd probably love it. Matching sweaters for every holiday.

ALEXIS Enters

ALEX   What the hell was that noise?

GERT   The car rolled into the garage door.

BEN   Grandma drove the car into the garage door.

GERT   (To BEN) Snitches get stitches.

ALEX   (To GERT) Did you get that outfit at T&A?

GERT   Yeah, you like?

ALEX   I tend not to shop there.

BEN   Why, because they don't sell flannels and jeans?

ALEX   I was going to say the stuff there looks a little tarty, but Gram, you pull that look off.

GERT   You think Barney will like it?

ALEX   I think you might give him a heart attack.

GERT   In a good way, or...?

ALEX   At Barney's age, I don't think any kind of heart attack is good.

GERT   I think he can handle it. Listen, can you kids cover for me while I go out the front? I'm going to walk to the bus station. Oh, and tell your mother not to wait up.

GERT Exits, grabbing a pair of stilettos from the shoe pile on her way out.

ALEX   Did Mom talk to Dad?

BEN   Yeah, just about how he's coming to drive me instead of flying.

ALEX   He didn't tell her your other thing?

BEN   Hell no.

ALEX   Don't you think you should?

BEN   Are you going to tell her your other thing?

ALEX   No, I don't think she's ready to hear it.

BEN	Well, I don't think she's ready to hear my thing either.
ALEX	I just don't want to upset her, not before I leave.
BEN	Me neither. I don't want to upset her.
ALEX	She's got enough to worry about with the car thing.
BEN	And the garage thing.
ALEX	And the grandmother thing.
BEN	And the Dad thing.
ALEX	Ok, so we both agree not to say anything yet.
BEN	Right.
ALEX	When the time is right, we'll know.
BEN	Sure.

Beat.

BEN	Do you think Grandma is going to get tired of Barney anytime soon?
ALEX	She always get tired of them, Ben. She's got the attention span of a middle school girl.
BEN	But she seems to like Barney more than the other old dudes.
ALEX	We thought the same thing about Clarence. And Eugene. And Norman.
BEN	I was surprised by Norman. For a guy with an oxygen tank, he was pretty spry.

FRANCINE Enters

FRAN	It's absolutely wrecked. I have no idea how we are go-

ing to afford paying to fix that. Mom, do you have any idea... Where's your grandmother?

ALEX   Hot date.

FRAN   Oh for Pete's sake. You two couldn't have stopped her?

BEN   I'm not about to tackle an old woman who likes to wear stilettos. I could get stabbed.

ALEX   Is the van ok at least?

FRAN   (letting out a sigh) She backed into the garage, so no engine damage. I guess just add it to the list of stuff to fix.

BEN   Hey, maybe dad could help fix it while he's here.

FRAN   Your father is many things, Ben. But a handyman he is not. This house is mostly held together by duct tape that your Dad used to fix everything. No, no. I am going to make sure this time your grandmother hires someone. I know she's squirreling away money to go to some music festival in the desert. She can use that money instead to help pay for the garage repair.

ALEX   Mom, do you think I can use the car tonight?

FRAN   What for?

ALEX   I have... I have a date.

FRAN   A date? Who's the lucky boy? Do I know him?

ALEX   I don't think you do.

FRAN   Well, I guess that will be ok. Just be careful. I saw this TV special about these men out there who pose as someone else on the internet and then boom, they kidnap you and bring you to a murder basement.

BEN	You don't have to worry about that with Alex.
ALEX	(Elbows BEN) Because I didn't meet my date on the internet.
FRAN	Well, good. Now, I have to go call the nursing home and make sure Grandma got there without setting anything on fire. Again.

FRANCINE grabs the phone and marches from the room.

BEN	I thought you did meet your date on the internet.
ALEX	It's a phone app, it's different. And if you give anything away to Mom, I am sure as shit going to tell her your little secret.
BEN	I won't give anything away. Have fun on your date. (Wiggles his eyebrows) Though why anyone would want to date you...
ALEX	(Flipping him the bird) Says the guy without a girlfriend.
BEN	You're going to miss me while you're in Scotland. Admit it.
ALEX	Never. Counting down the days 'til I don't have to see your face every day.
BEN	Oh yeah, you'll miss me.

BOTH Exit, arguing good-naturedly.

BLACKOUT

SCENE 2

The next morning.

FRANCINE is on the phone again.

FRAN   Hi, yes, finally. I have been on hold for a while now. They kept sending me to different customer service reps. My question is how much will it cost to FedEx a turkey to California. And can I use a flat rate box. No, this isn't a joke. My son is going across the country and he dropped the bombshell that he won't be home for Thanksgiving. So I am trying to figure out how to get food to him. Yes, it'll be cooked. I don't want him getting salmonella. Look, I know it's an unusual request but you see, his father and I are (whispers) divorced. Yes, and he has invited my son there for Thanksgiving and dropped another bombshell that my ex-husband has a girlfriend now. That I didn't know about. I mean, why wouldn't Carl have mentioned her before? If he'd just told me, I would have been fine with it. I want what's best for him. (Listens for a moment) Well, I don't know, Cheryl. I guess I want my ex to be happy. But I thought at least he'd have the decency to tell me he found someone else. No, no I am not harboring any lingering feelings.

ALEXIS Enters

        Sorry, Cheryl, I have to go. Thanks for your help.

ALEX   Who was that?

FRAN   Fedex. I'm going to ship Ben a turkey for Thanksgiving.

ALEX   I thought he was going to Dad's for the holidays.

FRAN   Well, your Dad doesn't know how to cook, and who knows about this mystery woman—

ALEX   Michelle.

FRAN   Michelle?

ALEX   Yeah. His girlfriend. He posts pictures and stuff of her on Facebook.

FRAN   Facebook?

ALEX   Yeah. I keep forgetting you aren't on it.

FRAN   My face is fine where it is. Does this Michelle cook?

ALEX   Not like you, I'm sure, Mom.

FRAN   (Placated) Oh, thank you, Sweetie.

ALEX   Besides, maybe I'm the one who you should be sending the turkey to. They don't even know what Thanksgiving is in Scotland.

FRAN   I know what I can do! I'll make a turkey this year for Christmas dinner. So you both can have some.

ALEX   (Looking apologetic) I meant to talk to you about that, Mom.

FRAN   Sweet baby Jesus, are you about to tell me you aren't coming home for Christmas this year?

ALEX   I didn't want to upset you. I was hoping that I could make it work, but I got my schedule, and the semester finals are two days before Christmas. And I signed up to do a January term with a few friends. So it doesn't make sense to come home only for a few days.

FRAN   But it's Christmas! We love Christmas!

ALEX	I know. I'm really going to miss you and your holiday traditions. But this is kind of my only chance to do this.
FRAN	I can't believe it.
ALEX	If it helps, I don't think Ben will be able to come back for Christmas either.
FRAN	That doesn't help! That's like squeezing lemon juice into my open wound! And then rubbing salt all over it.
ALEX	I'm sorry, Mom.
FRAN	Oh, God. What if you meet a man in Scotland, and you fall in love?
ALEX	Oh, come on, Mom.
FRAN	I've seen Scottish men. They're all rugged and handsome and they have those accents. You are going to marry a Scottish man and then you'll never come home to see me. You'll miss every holiday. And I'll have Scottish grandbabies and I'll have to move overseas if I ever want to see them and their little ginger heads.
ALEX	I can't tell if you're more upset about me missing holidays or me having red- headed children.
FRAN	A little of both. I don't know.
ALEX	Mom, seriously, you don't have to worry about that.
FRAN	You don't know. Love can strike anywhere.
ALEX	I won't fall for a Scottish man. I promise you that.
FRAN	My sweet twins. Gone, leaving me alone.

ALEX	You won't be alone. You have grandma Gertrude.
FRAN	At least I have her with me. Speaking of which, have you seen her this morning?
ALEX	I think she's already left.
FRAN	Left?
ALEX	Said she was going to the nursing home. Trolling for honeys, she said.
FRAN	What about Barney?
ALEX	Old news.
FRAN	They were dating the other day.
ALEX	You know her. She likes to love 'em and leave 'em.
FRAN	Another one bites the dust, then.
ALEX	Figuratively. I mean, I hope.
FRAN	My own mother is making me go gray. (Goes to her sewing machine) I have to get back to working on my next commission. I will probably be sewing all day. I have to pay for that garage door somehow.

Phone rings.

FRAN	Can you—
ALEX	Got it. (Picks up phone)
FRAN	If it's Cheryl at FedEx I'll take it.
ALEX	Hello? Hey Dad! You're breaking up a bit. What?
FRAN	Oh, can you ask him when next week he's leaving to come to get your brother?

ALEX	Mom asked when you are leaving. Already? (To FRAN) He's already on the road.
FRAN	(Rises from the sewing machine, hovers over her daughter) What? Already on the road?
ALEX	(Into Phone) When will you get here?
FRAN	I just talked to him yesterday. It's still August. Why is he already on his way?
ALEX	(To FRAN) Arriving in a few days.
FRAN	A few days?
ALEX	(Into Phone) Are you leaving right away, or are you staying around here for a bit?
FRAN	Did he get a hotel? There are no good hotels around here.
ALEX	(To Fran) Hotel.
FRAN	Which one, because the Barber Inn up the road has bedbugs.
ALEX	(Into Phone) Which one did you book?
FRAN	If he needs to, he can stay here. We have a guest room. And he is your father.
ALEX	(To Fran) He did have a booking with the Barber Inn. (Into phone) Mom says that you guys can stay here. She has the guest room.
FRAN	What do you mean "you guys?"
ALEX	(Still into the phone) Yeah, she offered. I can't wait to see you. It'll be great to catch up before I leave.
FRAN	What did you mean, "you guys?"

ALEX	Ok, I'll let her know. Text me pictures, ok?
FRAN	Who is "you guys?"
ALEX	(To Fran) Dad and Michelle. (Back to phone) Hey, can you put Michelle on the phone?
FRAN	Michelle? The girlfriend? She's with him?
ALEX	Yeah, they're coming together. You'll get to meet her. (Back into the phone) Michelle! Hey, girl! (ALEX exits, still talking on the phone.)

FRANCINE is left alone in the kitchen.

FRAN	Carl. And Michelle. Are coming here. To my house. In a few days. Ok. That's fine. That's fine.

There is a knock at the kitchen door. FRAN goes to it, in a daze, and opens it to reveal HANK. He wears a tool belt. Francine looks him up and down.

HANK	Hey. Is this where Gertrude Waldroop lives?
FRAN	Oh, God, her boyfriends. They keep getting younger.
HANK	Excuse me?
FRAN	You're here to see Gertrude?
HANK	Yeah, she gave me a call. I guess she looked at my website and liked my stuff.
FRAN	My mom went on a website to find you?
HANK	Yeah. She mentioned on the phone she liked the pictures of other things I'd done. So she hired me.
FRAN	Hired? You're getting paid?
HANK	Well, what I do isn't for free.

FRAN   Jesus, Mom.

HANK   She sent me pictures, too.

FRAN   Oh no.

HANK   I assessed the damage, and it'll be about $600.

FRAN   She agreed to pay you that?

HANK   I mean, I bring my own hardware.

FRAN   Oh, Jesus, Mary and Joseph.

HANK   I took another look on my way in. I can get started right now.

FRAN   She's not here. And I can't imagine she'll want you to get started without her.

HANK   Look, if you don't want me to fix the door, that's fine. I was just under the impression Gertrude wanted the garage fixed in the next few days.

FRAN   (Realizes her mistake) Oh, Heavens. You really are a handyman?

HANK   What else would I be?

FRAN   I thought you were an exotic dancer.

HANK   Not a great multitasker, I'm afraid. Just fix stuff.

FRAN   I am so sorry. I didn't know Mom—I didn't realize Gertrude called someone about the garage.

HANK   She knows my Father.

FRAN   Oh, dear, is your father Barney?

HANK   No.

FRAN   That's a mercy anyhow.

HANK   So, if you don't mind, I can get working on the garage door?

FRAN   Sure, sure. Um, $600 you said, right?

HANK   Yeah. That's the estimate. If there ends up being structural damage to the garage, I'll let you know before I continue.

FRAN   Oh, good.

HANK   Can I access the space above the garage?

FRAN   Yes. There's an apartment over it.

HANK   Occupied?

FRAN   No. Not yet. There's work that has to be done on the sink and shower up there, so I haven't been able to rent it yet.

HANK   Ok. I might have to go up there to get to the electric. But I'll let you know.

FRAN   Thanks. I'll be here. (Rambling) I mean, not just in the kitchen, I have other rooms. Obviously. But I mostly work in the kitchen. So just let yourself in if you need anything. Though I might take a shower later. If I do that, I'll lock the door, so you don't come right in. But you can ring the bell. My daughter and son are here, so they can let you in if you need to get in. But I'll probably be here.

HANK   Good to know. (HANK Exits)

FRAN   (Back to the sewing machine) You need to learn to stop rambling, Francine Peters. (Slumps a little) Francine Waldroop.

GERTRUDE tries to slip into the kitchen from outside unnoticed.

FRAN   (not turning) I can hear your jingling earrings from here, Mom.

GERT   Oh, hey, Francie.

FRAN   (Turning) Where have you been, young lady?

GERT   I was volunteering at the nursing home.

FRAN   Volunteering? As what?

GERT   Yoga instructor.

FRAN   You don't know yoga.

GERT   But I know how to stretch those gentlemen out.

FRAN   Why are you like this?

GERT   I am merely trying to enjoy what remains of my life.

FRAN   Stop acting like you're on your death bed.

GERT   You never know, sweetie. I might not make it to Christmas.

FRAN   You wouldn't be the only one.

GERT   What?

FRAN   The kids.

GERT   The kids aren't coming for the holidays?

FRAN   Apparently not. You know how I love celebrating every little thing. Now there are going to be big gaps. I can't enjoy the holidays if they aren't going to be here.

GERT	You always find a way to celebrate, dear. I'm sure you'll come up with something.
FRAN	On top of that, Carl and his girlfriend are coming to pick up Ben. They're already on their way.
GERT	Carl's got a girl, huh?
FRAN	Yeah. Michelle.
GERT	Looks like you're the only one not getting any.
FRAN	Mom.
GERT	Sorry, sweetie. Maybe you need some yoga, it'll relax you.
FRAN	Do you know any moves?
GERT	None I'd be willing to show you.
FRAN	Gross. But that reminds me. Your handyman is here.
GERT	Oh, good. Wasn't sure when to expect him.
FRAN	He said you knew his father. Did you... teach him yoga?
GERT	Walter? Oh, no. Walter's not like that.
FRAN	Walter?
GERT	He just recently moved into the nursing home. And he teases me for going on all these dates. He's so... he's so... I can't even describe him. He's always got this smirk, like he's judging me when I come in, wearing my Saturday Best.
FRAN	So you don't like him?
GERT	Oh, no, not at all.

FRAN   And yet you called his son to come fix the garage?

GERT   I just remembered Walter telling me his son was new in town. And that he is a contractor. So I Googled him. And he's good at his job. Why, don't you like him?

FRAN   He seems fine. I mean, considering I thought he was an exotic dancer.

GERT   Is he that good looking? I mean, Walter's a looker, so his son must be.

FRAN   Oh, so Walter's handsome?

GERT   Objectively. Not my type, though. He's the bad boy of the nursing home.

FRAN   What, does he steal extra Jell-O when the nurses' backs are turned?

GERT   Heck no. They have great food there. Why do you think I date so many men from Shady Acres? They have top notch cuisine. And don't get me started on the thread- count on those sheets...

FRAN   I don't want to think about how you know about the sheets there. You're talking like you want to go there.

GERT   There's worse ways to spend infirmity.

FRAN   You're kidding, right? You're not going to admit your-self one these days, and not come back?

GERT   If you keep giving me the third degree every time I try to leave, I might.

FRAN   Your threats won't work on me.

GERT   I don't have to take this.

FRAN   Oh yes you do, as long as you are under my roof. Now... got to your room.

GERT   What, am I grounded now?

FRAN   I don't know how else to handle you. You're like a teenager.

GERT   Well, fine. I'll go to my room. But I ain't giving you my savings for that garage door. If you're the grown-up here, you pay for it. That money I'm saving? I'm keeping it. I'm going to Coachella, and you're not stopping me.

GERT storms out of the room.

FRAN   (After her, as Hank enters the back door.) Careful, if you storm out that fast again you might leave your dentures behind you!

HANK   I said the same thing to my Dad just the other day.

FRAN   Oh, you're here. You're back. Sorry.

HANK   No need to apologize.

FRAN   Sorry.

HANK   Is there an echo in here?

FRAN   How did the door look?

HANK   I took a look up in the apartment above, it looks like the electrical for the garage door was all duct taped together.

FRAN   Sounds about right. My husband... Ex-husband. That would be his calling card.

HANK   I'm surprised it hasn't caused some issues in the past.

Like, catching the garage on fire. It looked like it was kind of half-assed. Pardon my French.

FRAN   No, it's ok. Carl half-assed most things.

HANK   Well, the estimate is going to go up just a bit. $800 should do it.

FRAN $800. Ok. Um.

HANK   Something wrong?

FRAN   Just, that's a lot of money. I don't have that money right now.

HANK   You don't have to pay me up front. You can pay me when the work is done.

FRAN   Well, I don't know if I'll have the money later, either.

HANK   Where I used to live, I did work for barter sometimes.

FRAN   I'm a tailor. I don't suppose you need anything hemmed? Or tailored? Or altered?

HANK   I usually just buy clothes that fit me.

FRAN   (Getting a little frazzled) Oh, dear. Well, um, I think I might be able to take something down to the pawn shop. Oh, but what if they don't take any of my jewelry? Knowing Carl, most of the gold he'd gotten me over the years was probably duct tape painted yellow. I'll not be able to pay, and then the garage will be wide open to the elements. We'll get raccoons. Or vagabonds. They'll start squatting, and I'll have to go to court, which will cost even more money—

HANK   Now, don't go getting carried away. Maybe take a breath.

FRAN   (Taking several breaths, smooshing her face in her hands. She glances around the room, and repeats as she sees things) Table, Chairs, Sewing machine, handyman, tool belt. (She calms down) Phew, ok. There we are.

HANK   You alright?

FRAN   Yes. Sometimes I get a little overwhelmed with the world, and I have to ground myself by naming five things that I see.

HANK   Well, if it helps in the future, my name is Hank. Then you can name me by name, not my occupation.

FRAN   Hank. I'm Francine. Thank you. I am sorry about panicking. And the whole vagabond thing.

HANK   I've seen worse. Look, how about this. I do the work now, and you pay me when you can. My Dad always has good things to say about your mother. Gertrude, right? He wouldn't want you risking... vagabonds and raccoons.

FRAN   I couldn't do that to you. You're new here. You can't go around giving out free work. How would you pay rent?

HANK   I don't pay rent. I'm living at the Barber Inn, until I find a place.

FRAN   The Barber Inn?

HANK   Yeah, it's cheap.

FRAN   That's because they have bedbugs.

HANK   Bedbugs? Shit. Pardon my French.

FRAN   No, it's ok. It is shit. You can't seriously be living there.

HANK   I sold my other place. I wanted to be closer to Dad, now that he's in the nursing home.

FRAN   So you don't have anywhere to sleep?

HANK   Now that I know there are bedbugs, I guess the floor at the Inn will be my bed.

FRAN   Oh! Bartering! You said you could barter, right? You need a bed! I have a bed!

HANK   Are you offering to share?

FRAN   Share? My bed? (Giggles nervously) No, no, no. That would be silly. No, you could stay in the apartment above the garage. For as long as you need, rent free. If you fix the garage. You can stay in the apartment while you look for something more permanent.

HANK   Don't you want to rent it to a paying tenant?

FRAN   Well, at some point. But it's not really livable now. Which reminds me. If you want to live in it, you'll have to use our shower for the time being. Until it's fixed.

HANK   I am a contractor. I think I can manage to fix it up a bit. Then, when I leave, it'll be ready for you to rent.

FRAN   That would be so great.

HANK   Alright. I guess we have a deal, then. I'll write up a contract and bring it over tomorrow, with some of my stuff.

FRAN   Oh, you probably have to get all of your things fumigated. And possibly yourself. Bedbugs, you know.

HANK   Right. Well, it was good to meet you, Francine. I'll be back tomorrow.

FRAN   Great, I'll be here. Well, maybe not here, here. I might be out shopping. Or, I could be dropping something off to a client. You know how it is. Maybe. In any case, if I'm not here, I'll leave the key for you. But it'll be hidden, so no one else can find it. You know, like under a mat or something. But I'll leave a note about where I hide it.

HANK tries to edge himself out as she rambles.

FRAN   Let me just come out with you and show you where I am going to hide the note about the key.

HANK and FRAN exit, lights down.

SCENE 3

The next morning.

FRAN is sitting at the table wearing a Christmas sweater. There is a small Christmas tree on the table. There is a wreath hanging on the door to the outside. She is happily cutting out paper snowflakes.

ALEXIS and BEN enter, wearing pajamas. They stop, seeing their mother at the table.

FRAN   Well, Good morning, my dears! And Merry Christmas!

ALEXIS   Mom, it's August.

BEN   Oh no, she's finally gone off the deep end. I knew this would happen.

FRAN   I know it's August, you silly. Wait, what do you mean you knew I would go off the deep end?

ALEXIS   What are you doing with all of this Christmas stuff, Mom?

FRAN   Well, this morning while I was in the attic getting out the suitcases for you both, I saw all of our Christmas decorations. And it just made me so sad to think of you both being away for the holidays this year. So I thought that I would just have a little Christmas in August for us! So we can celebrate early. Come on, come sit. I made some cinnamon buns, like we usually have for Christmas morning.

ALEX   Mom, are you sure you're ok?

FRAN   Of course. I just wanted to spend some time doing something fun with you both. I promise I'm not crazy.

GERT   (Enters, looks around, shakes her head sadly) She's finally gone off the deep end.

FRAN   Mom! No, I haven't gone off the deep end. Now, come have Christmas breakfast.

GERT   It's not December right now, is it? Did I slip into a coma?

FRAN   Sorry, not all Christmas wishes come true.

ALEX   This is a nice idea, Mom. (Walks to the table, sits as FRAN places a cinnamon bun down in front of her)

BEN   I do love the cinnamon buns you make, Ma. (He sits)

GERT   Kids, stop feeding into her delusions!

FRAN   Mom, you want a bun?

GERT   (Thinks.) Alright, fine. I guess we're just steering into the skid here. (Sits down)

FRAN   (Settling back into her chair) See? Isn't this nice? Just the family, spending time together? This will almost make up for not seeing you for Thanksgiving and Christmas.

ALEX   I wish I'd known about this ahead of time. I would have gotten you all a Christmas present.

FRAN   You can both just bring me a present in February.

ALEX   February?

BEN   February?

FRAN   Sure. When you come home for your birthdays.

BEN and ALEXIS share a look. FRAN catches it.

FRAN   Sweet Mary Mother of Pearl. Are you telling me you aren't coming home for your birthday either?

BEN   Well, I was thinking of spending it with Dad.

ALEX   I figure I will probably want to go out with people in my school program.

FRAN   Ok, so what about April break?

BEN   I am going to visit cousin Jake and Will in April in Washington. I promised them.

ALEX   The school years in Scotland are different. They don't have a break in April.

FRAN   Ok, so when exactly are my children going to be coming home again?

BEN and ALEXIS share a look.

ALEX & BEN (Together) August?

FRAN stands up from her chair.

FRAN   (Flabbergasted) Next... Next August? As in, a year from now? A whole YEAR?

GERT   It must be that time during Christmas where everyone starts fighting.

FRAN   You are leaving me for a whole year?

ALEX   I didn't realize it would make you so upset.

FRAN   How could it not make me upset? You're my babies!

BEN   We just figured that you would be glad to have us out of the house for the first time in years.

ALEX   Yeah, so you could have some time to yourself.

FRAN   Time... to myself? What the heck am I supposed to do all by myself?

BEN   Take up a hobby or something. Like ballroom dancing.

ALEX   Or roller derby.

GERT   Or getting a boyfriend.

FRAN   I think I might have a panic attack again.

ALEX   Mom, deep breaths.

BEN   Five things in the room, Ma.

GERT   Think happy thoughts.

FRAN   (Breathing) Five things. Five things. Christmas tree. Snowflake. Cinnamon bun. Children. Abandonment.

ALEX   Did that help?

FRAN   Not really. I can't believe you are leaving me for that long.

BEN   We will call you whenever we can.

ALEX   And I can send you videos.

GERT   And you can come see me at the nursing home whenever you want. Just call first.

FRAN   Mom, you're not going anywhere.

GERT   Just seeing if I could sneak that in there.

FRAN   You are both going to miss so much. We will miss Thanksgiving, Christmas, your birthdays... the fourth of July! Grandparents Day!

GERT   Hey, we've never celebrated that before.

FRAN   Well, this would be a good time to start.

ALEX   But Mom, we are having Christmas right now. We can celebrate now, can't we?

FRAN   But what about the other holidays? What about our traditions?

BEN   I'm sure we can celebrate in new ways this year. You are super crafty, Mom. You can come up with something fun, like the way you did today. Alexis and I can send you care packages in the mail for each holiday or something.

ALEX   Yeah, we will make up new traditions.

Phone starts to ring. FRAN, in her alarmed state, ignore it.

BEN   I'll get it. (Grabs the phone)

ALEX   Mom? We are going to miss you, you know?

GERT   The kiddos are growing up, Francie. It happens!

BEN   Hello? Oh, hey Dad.

FRAN snaps her head around.

BEN   You want to talk to Mom? Uh... (Glances at FRAN, who is panic stricken.)

FRAN   Tablecloth, fork, tree, snowflake, children growing up too fast...

BEN   Yeah, now's not really a great time. She's feeling emotional about us leaving so soon. Oh, already? Um, ok, I'll let her know. Yeah, ok.

ALEXIS hops up, tries to take the phone.

ALEX   Wait, can I talk to Michelle?

BEN   Hey, Alexis wants to talk to Shelley. Can you put her on?

FRAN   Shelley? You have a nickname for her already?

ALEX   (into phone) Hi, Shelley! Can't wait to finally meet you in person! (She wanders out of the room, talking)

FRAN   This is all too much right now.

HANK appears at the kitchen door, knocks.

FRAN   (Jumping out of her chair) Oh, dear, is it Carl already with Shelley?

GERT   (Going to the door) You need valium, Francie. (lets Hank into the kitchen) Hi, Hank. How's it going? Good to see you again.

HANK   Hi Mrs. Waldroop.

GERT   Please, call me Lucinda.

FRAN   Mom, your name is Gertrude.

GERT   She's always raining on my parade.

HANK   My father sends his best wishes, Gertrude.

GERT   He's not dead yet?

HANK	Still kicking.
GERT	Humph. Handsome as ever, I suppose?
HANK	He's a stylish guy. Not unlike yourself.
GERT	You got his charm, that's for sure. Damn, if I were ten years younger...
FRAN	You mean forty years.
GERT	(Shaking her head, elbowing Hank) See? (Miming) Parade? Rain. (Returns to her seat at the table with Ben, who is cutting out snowflakes.)
HANK	Sorry to interrupt breakfast.
FRAN	Oh, we weren't having breakfast, we were having a crisis.
HANK	I hear that goes well with bacon. Or, in this case, Christmas Cheer. What happened here, did Santa have a mid-summer rave?
FRAN	We are celebrating a little early this year, that's all.
HANK	And here I forgot my ugly Christmas sweater. I see you have yours, though.
FRAN	(offended) What do you mean, ugly?
HANK	Ahem, nothing. I brought my stuff. I just wanted to let you know in case you hear bumping around up-stairs.
GERT	When the upstairs is bumping, don't come---
FRAN	Mother.
GERT	I didn't realize you were going to be a new tenant.

BEN	In the apartment? It's fixed up?
FRAN	No, but it will be. Thanks to Hank.
HANK	Hank Williams. Nice to meet you.
GERT	Like the country singer.
HANK	The only singing I do is in the shower. Which, is another annoying sound you might hear now that I'm moving in.
BEN	Mom sings in the shower, too.
FRAN	(Laughing) Oh, well, maybe we'll harmonize, Hank. I mean, from separate showers. You know. I'll be in one. You'll be in the other. I mean, you probably won't even be able to hear me, because of the water on your head and your body and all that. Not that I'll be actively listening for you or anything, either. You know. Just...
HANK	I got it.
FRAN	(nervous laugh) Oh, good. You stopped me.
HANK	In any case, After I move things upstairs, I'll get to work on the garage door. (Starts to open the door, the handle comes off)
FRAN	Oh... I'm sorry about that. Duct tape. It's all over the place.
HANK	If you ever need help with things like this, I am your guy. I can come back later and screw this into place.
FRAN	You're my guy? My screw guy. Well, great. I mean, you know what I mean. But yes. Please help. Everything is falling apart.

HANK	Later, then. (HANK shakes his head, amused, and leaves)
GERT	Yikes.
BEN	And I thought teenagers were awkward.
FRAN	Oh, shush. I wasn't awkward. Was I? Was that terribly awkward?
GERT	Is the Pope Catholic?
BEN	Did you hire him or rent the apartment to him?
FRAN	Both.
GERT	She's putting all her eggs into one basket.
FRAN	That doesn't even make sense.
GERT	He's cute, though.
FRAN	Is he? I didn't notice.
BEN	Mom. You noticed.
FRAN	What?
BEN	I am pretty sure you were flirting. Cringey as it might have been.
FRAN	No, I have never flirted a day in my life. Not even with your father. I don't flirt.
BEN	You do now. (Takes his cinnamon bun and starts from the room) I gotta go pack, Mom. But thanks for Christmas. It was a nice gesture. (Kisses her on the cheek, then exits)
GERT	Since you're in the Christmas Spirit, would you mind dropping me off at the nursing home, sweetie?

FRAN   But you broke up with Barney.

GERT   Today is Open House at Shady Acres. That means it's going to be open season for fresh meat.

FRAN   Why are you like this?

GERT   (Shrugging) Gotta keep young somehow.

FRAN   Fine. I'll drive you.

GERT   Oh, but you have to change before we go. I can't be seen with a fuddy-duddy like you. They'll think I'm admitting you.

FRAN and GERT Exit.

SCENE 4

A new day.

A large paper clock with moveable hands has been stuck to the fridge. Gold and black sparkling décor is draped around the room. Plastic Champagne flutes are stacked on the counter with a bottle of sparkling grape juice. There are also some anachronistic birthday presents and a "Happy 19th Birthday" sign with party hats on the table. To really sell the "New Years Eve" theme, FRAN enters on the phone, wearing a top hat. She is flipping through a magazine as she talks on the phone and walks.

FRAN   (Humming 'Auld Lang Sine" to herself. Suddenly into the phone) Yes, hi! Finally. I keep getting connected to different departments. I am trying to see if you have some decorations in stock. (Listens, gesturing to the magazine as if they can see it) It's all listed right here in the catalogue from last year. I need to order one large Easter Bunny, and several packages of the plastic eggs you stuff with candy. And also three of those pink heart-shaped baskets for Valentine's day. And a dozen of the— (Cut off; looking offended.) Yes, I am well aware that it's August. I need these things for a party. Yes, all together. Listen, my children are leaving for college, and they won't be home. And we only have a few more days until they are out of my house and I won't see them for a whole year. So we need to pick up the pace and celebrate a few of the holidays together. (Listens) What do you mean you don't have the Easter bunny in stock? Can't you check clearance? No, I am not hysterical.

As FRAN yelps into the phone, ALEXIS and BEN Enter, carrying bags.

FRAN   I need the four-foot tall Easter bunny and forty-eight plastic eggs and a dozen of your American flag banners!! (Seeing the children enter) Gotta go. (Hangs up the phone) Customer service isn't what it used to be. Hello, my children! Or should I say, Happy Birthday New Years!

BEN   (Looking around the room) It's like Party City barfed in here.

ALEX   Mom, you are looking…festive.

BEN   We aren't going to be 19 for several more months, Mom.

FRAN   I seem to have miscalculated how many holidays we need to get through. So I am combining a few of them. (Picks up sheets from the table) I even made schedules, like a cruise director. So now you know what holiday to expect. (Hands the schedules out to BEN and ALEX)

BEN   (Reading schedule) New Years and our birthday. I like that combo.

FRAN   Oh, and we need to celebrate in style! (Hands them each a birthday hat and a New Years top hat. She tries to stack them both on their heads simultaneously.) You can switch back and forth. And we have got to have some champagne to celebrate. (Pours into the glasses, hands them to the kids)

ALEX   Champagne?

GERT   (Entering from interior. Today Gert is dressed in aerobics gear, tight and bright.) Sounds like my kind of breakfast.

FRAN   It's not real champagne. You two are still underage.

ALEX   I won't be underage in Scotland.

FRAN   It's also ten in the morning.

GERT   It's five o'clock somewhere.

BEN   What do we toast to?

FRAN   Your birthday. Here's to my little babies growing up so fast.

GERT   When are we going to celebrate Grandparent's Day?

FRAN   Check the schedule. I think I was able to squeeze it in, Mom.

GERT   (Takes a schedule) Hm. You are doubling up on some of these.

BEN   Mom didn't realize how many holidays are in the year.

FRAN   We celebrate most of these, anyway.

GERT   Arbor Day?

FRAN   Celebrate trees and nature.

GERT   Groundhog day?

FRAN   I found one of the kids' old beaver hand-puppets, I was going to repurpose it.

ALEX   I think maybe we should skip Cinco De Mayo, Mom. We're not Mexican.

GERT   I sure as shit am not going to be celebrating "Tax

Day".

FRAN   Ok, so maybe I got a little carried away. But we definitely have to celebrate the big ticket items.

ALEX   I will be back down in a few, Mom. I have to run my new books upstairs. (Exits)

FRAN   Ben, did you get all your books too? I am going to ship Alex's to Scotland, I can do the same for you so you don't have to lug them all in your suitcase.

BEN   (Evasive) Oh, no I didn't get mine yet. I think I am just going to buy mine when I get out to California.

FRAN   Oh, but you might be able to get them cheaper here.

BEN   It'll be fine.

FRAN   But did you get things for your dorm room? Or school supplies?

BEN   No, I just got some new clothes. It'll be hotter there, you know.

FRAN   Don't put off getting school stuff too long, honey. You can't be there on the first day of your classes and not have a notebook and paper!

BEN   Right. I'll get around to it. I'm going to bring my new clothes upstairs. I'll show them to you, later, ok?

FRAN   Sounds good. Go get your sister, and come back down. I want you two to open your birthday presents!

BEN   Will do, Mom. (Exits)

GERT   (Doing some warm up stretches) Don't you think you're making them a little crazy with all this holiday stuff?

FRAN   Crazy? Of course not. They had so much fun yesterday when we celebrated Saint Patrick's Day and Boxing Day! Corned beef hash and punching the punching bag.

GERT   I don't think you know what Boxing Day is.

FRAN   Halloween and Fourth of July will be tomorrow. You'll like that one.

GERT   Do we all have to dress up like Founding Fathers? Because that feels more like a President's Day gag.

FRAN   I have a whole other thing planned for Presidents' Day. We are going to play, "Match the President to the Contribution to America" and wear Martin Van Buren sideburns.

GERT   (Looking stricken) Francie. I was kidding. I don't think we need to celebrate Presidents' Day.

FRAN   Well, how else am I supposed to spend these next days? Worrying about the kids? Fretting over what I will do in this empty house when they are gone?

GERT   You could, I dunno, spend time with your kids like a normal human being?

FRAN   No, no. We have always had activities to do. They don't like spending time with me when we just... sit. I can't just sit. Because if I sit, I think. And if I think, I worry. And if I worry, I panic. I panic about things like what if Ben gets a face tattoo and starts acting in Porn? And what if Alexis joins a Scottish cult and has to murder someone for her cult initiation? No, sitting always leads to panic. This way is better. Then I get to make so many memories. And it will tide me over for the year while they are away, making memories without me.

GERT   You don't have an off switch, huh?

FRAN   No.

GERT   I don't think the kids would mind just sitting and talking to you, instead of playing your Find the Four Leaf Clover scavenger hunt.

FRAN   Do you enjoy sitting and talking to me?

GERT   Sure.

FRAN   Well... do you want to sit and talk now?

GERT   Can't. Got a date.

FRAN   Oh, what else is new.

GERT   It's a date with Doris and Betty. We are going to go do jazzercise. Doris is picking me up.

FRAN   Oh. I'm surprised.

GERT   Why, because you didn't think I could do this? (Demonstrates some Jazzercise)

FRAN   No. Because I would have thought you'd be heading to the nursing home to scope out some hotties. Or you'd be getting picked up by Herb in his Cadillac Deville. Or hitchhiking to the Old Country Buffet to see what octogenarian men are hitting up the early bird specials.

GERT   That is rude, and I am offended. I am not all about men.

FRAN   That is literally all you are about.

GERT   Well, it just so happens that I have other interests outside of men.

FRAN   I'm sorry, Mom. I didn't mean to assume. I know you have a lot of interests.

GERT   Good. Besides, it doesn't hurt that the park where we do our jazzercise is right next to the gentlemen's shuffleboard tournament.

FRAN   Of course it is.

GERT   Have a Merry New Birthday Kwanza or whatever. I'll be back.

FRAN   You can't escape all my holidays!

GERT   (Headed to kitchen door. Doesn't see Hank on the other side of the glass as she turns back to FRAN) You know, there is one holiday I could get behind.

FRAN   Really? What's that?

GERT   Mardi Gras! (She turns and flashes FRAN, and, by accident, the kitchen door. HANK on the other side of the door looks shocked. He quickly moves out of sight again.) Now throw me a necklace.

FRAN   (Tosses GERT a necklace from a pile on the counter.) I guess I should be thankful I am the one you flashed today.

GERT   The day's still young, baby! (GERT waltzes out of the kitchen door).

FRAN   (Turning back to the kitchen, filled with decorations. It's a lonely place now that everyone is gone.) I guess I could try sitting. (She sits at the table for a minute, looking uncomfortable, and unable to stop herself from rearranging things.) Gosh, this is so hard. I feel like there's a million things I should be doing instead. No, no, I can do this. (Sits another minute.) What am I going to do when the kids are gone? Am I going to turn into Mrs. Havisham, just sitting in my old wedding dress, dusty and covered in cobwebs? Oh no. The panic is setting in.

HANK enters, quietly, with a tool kit.

FRAN   Everyone is going to move out. I am going to die alone. And even the cat won't care I'm dead. No, she'll half eat me. No one will find my body for weeks. And no one will come to my funeral, because my kids won't know, because no one will know how to get in touch with them. Oh, no. (Head in hands)

HANK   Might be a good idea to name five things you see.

FRAN   (Jumps a little, but nods) Right. Right. Presents. Top hat. Clock. Doorknob. Hank. (Seems to let out a sigh, calming down) Hank. Hi. Sorry. You caught me mid-panic.

HANK   You did a good job getting out of that one.

FRAN   I didn't hear you come in.

HANK   I imagine that was on account of the panic. Hope I didn't alarm you.

FRAN   No, no.

HANK   I noticed the water in my bathroom has almost no pressure. Thought I could check yours too, see if it's a house-wide problem or just the apartment.

FRAN   Oh. That's so thoughtful. Thank you.

HANK   Well, you can't shower without water pressure. And I wouldn't want to miss you shower singing. (He starts fiddling with the kitchen sink.)

FRAN (Mortified) Oh, sweet Mary Mother. You could hear me after all?

HANK (Smiling) A little bit.

FRAN I am so embarrassed.

HANK Don't be.

FRAN I don't even realize I'm doing it. I can't remember what I was singing.

HANK Hank Williams, funny enough.

FRAN No, really?

HANK "I'm so lonesome I could cry."

FRAN Oh, dear.

HANK Yeah, seems as though your water pressure is fine. I'll have to go tinker with the sink up there. Might be leak somewhere.

FRAN I hope not. That would just cause even more problems. Problems that duct tape won't fix.

HANK Duct tape really doesn't fix much.

FRAN Wish it could have fixed my marriage! Ha! (Forced laugh)

HANK Didn't fix mine, either.

FRAN Oh, you were married?

HANK We were high school sweethearts. She was head cheerleader.

FRAN   Aw. Were you the quarterback?

HANK   No, but that's who she ended up leaving me for.

FRAN   Yikes.

HANK   Yeah. (Glances at the décor) New Years and... birthday today?

FRAN   Yes. It's... dumb.

HANK   No, I like it.

FRAN   You do?

HANK   Yeah.

FRAN   It's not... crazy?

HANK   Oh, no, it's crazy.

FRAN   Oh.

HANK   But I like it.

FRAN   Oh.

HANK   It's nice to see how much you care about your kids, enough that you want them to have all these experiences that they are going to miss while they are away.

FRAN   I honestly don't know if I'm doing it for them... or if it's me being selfish and doing it because if I am focused on all this, then I don't have time to be sad.

HANK   You're a special kind of person, Francine. I think—

Phone rings.

FRAN   Oh, I'm sorry. I have to take this. I have a call into an Easter Bunny guy. (Grabs phone.) Hello? Oh, hi

Joe. (Smacks forehead) Joe! Right! No, no of course I didn't forget. Yes. Mmhm. I used the measurements you gave me, yes, but you are going to have to stay for a fitting, we have to make sure it'll fit right. By this afternoon? One? And you really can't stay for a fitting? No, I can make it work. I just need... (Spots Hank, gestures for him to stay as he starts for the door) No problem at all, Joe. It'll be good to go when you get here. Thanks, Joe. Bye bye. (Hangs up the phone)

HANK   Everything ok?

FRAN   The panic is a little high again.

HANK   What's wrong?

FRAN   See, I forgot one of my tailoring clients is coming to pick up today. Joe gave me the measurements, but I had hoped I could get in one last fitting. And the show Joe needs it for is tonight.

HANK   And Joe doesn't have time for a fitting?

FRAN   Exactly. The show is a big deal, really a black tie kind of affair.

HANK   Anything I can do to help?

FRAN   In fact, yes. I need you to try on the outfit. You and Joe are the exact same size.

HANK   How do you know that.

FRAN   I have an eye for it. (Looks Hank up and down, realizes what she is doing, and shakes her head) Not that I've been checking you out.

HANK   Likewise.

FRAN   What?

HANK   Nothing.

FRAN   Do you think you'd be able to try it on?

HANK   If it'll help you... Sure. Just be forewarned, black tie is not really my usual look. So it probably won't look right on me.

FRAN   Don't worry. It's not that kind of black tie. (Retrieves a garment bag, points to the bathroom) You can change in there.

HANK   Ok. (Exits with garment bag).

FRAN   (Calls into bathroom) Thank you for doing this for me, Hank.

HANK   Not a problem... (Pokes his head out) This is the right bag for Joe, right?

FRAN   Yes. Oh, jeez, I really hope it works. It would ruin my seamstress reputation if Joe gets up in front of all those people in something that looks horrible. It's so lucky you happened to be around right when I needed you. I mean, I could've had Ben try it on, but he's not the right size. He and Alexis are usually my models for things I make.

HANK   (From in the bathroom) So you tailor things that are already made. Do you ever make things from scratch?

FRAN   Oh, yes. (Unconsciously as she talks, she sits, doesn't fidget, and is still) I have come up with so many original designs. I love just going into a store and feeling all the fabrics. I love touching the different materials and imagining how it would be as a dress or shirt or outfit. I never use a pattern. I have always been able to see something in the flat fabric, to understand where I need to cut and where I need to gather and stitch and trim to make something whole and beautiful. And I like to take all the random little scraps, things that seem small, insignificant, like you can't use them. And I combine them and sew them together to make a whole new fabric. It's a tapestry of colors and patterns, that shouldn't go together, but somehow do. They start as little scraps, but in the end they make something... complete. (A little content sigh)

HANK   (After a pause) I like hearing you talk.

FRAN   You do?

HANK   You seem to love what you do.

FRAN   I do. I really do. If only it would pay the bills. Or, pay the handyman.

HANK   I'm just glad I'm not sleeping at the foot of my dad's bed. Or sharing a bed with his roommate, Chuck.

FRAN   Ah, Chuck. I believe my mom shared a bed with him.

HANK   My Dad talks a lot about your Mom, you know. For someone who claims to not like her tight clothes.

FRAN   My Mom talks a lot about your Dad, too. For someone who claims to not like his bad boy reputation.

HANK   Maybe he'd change his mind if he knew about Chuck, though.

FRAN   (Laughs) You know. This is the longest time I've just sat down and talked today.

HANK   That's better than sheer panic. Speaking of which. I think it's my turn to panic. I think you may have left something out about this.

FRAN   What?

HANK enters in a spectacularly gaudy drag queen gown, head to toe sparkle and feathers. He has a resigned look on his face.

HANK   You sure you gave me the right bag?

FRAN   Oh, that looks... perfect! Oh, Joe will be so excited.

HANK   What kind of performance is Joe attending tonight?

FRAN   Oh, Joe's not just attending. Joe goes by the stage name Joanna Bang. She's the main stage act at Drag King Con tonight.

HANK   Bang?

FRAN   Yeah, like a gun, "Bang, Bang."

HANK   Pretty sure it's a different kind of bang.

FRAN   A different kind?

HANK   Joanna Bang?

FRAN   Oh my goodness. I just realized how that sounds. Heavens.

HANK   Couldn't fit in the shoes. But surprisingly this doesn't look bad with the work- boots.

FRAN   It's fantastic, isn't it?

HANK   It's a work of art.

FRAN   I am pretty proud of this one. Now, if you don't mind, I need to make a few alterations.

HANK   Whatever you need.

FRAN	(Using pins to adjust here, a tape to measure there.) So, how long ago did you get divorced.
HANK	Six years.
FRAN	Four for me.
HANK	It gets easier.
FRAN	I hope so. I think I am past the worst of it.
HANK	How did your kids handle it?
FRAN	As well as can be expected, I think. They were kind of their own people by then. Alexis said she had a feeling it was coming. And Ben said whatever makes us happiest.
HANK	You have a couple good kids, sounds like. They seem well-adjusted.
FRAN	Thank you. Do you have any children?
HANK	No, wish I did. Kim didn't want them, so I didn't want to push it.
FRAN	That's a pity. You seem like the type who'd make a good dad.
HANK	Because I am handy around the house?
FRAN	No, because I asked you to put on a dress and you did it. When Alexis used to ask to paint her Daddy's toenails or do his hair, he'd say no.
HANK	This is different, though.
FRAN	You think?
HANK	Yeah. Because I look fabulous in this color.

FRAN   You're not wrong.

GERT enters through the kitchen door.

GERT   It's hot as hell out there. Way too hot to be doing jazzercise, I'll tell you that right now.

FRAN   What, you didn't pick up any gents on your way?

GERT   Pickin's were slim. (Sizing up HANK) Damn.

HANK   Is that a good damn?

GERT   You bet your sweet bippy it is. That really hugs all your assets.

HANK   You'll make me blush.

GERT   Francie, Sweetie, you really outdid yourself on this piece.

FRAN   Thanks, Mom.

GERT   You changing careers, Hank?

HANK   Do Drag Queens get good dental insurance? Because in that case, I might.

FRAN   But then who would fix up this money pit of a house?

HANK   Fair point.

GERT   Hank, has your father kicked the bucket yet?

HANK   Not so far as I know.

GERT   Damn shame.

HANK   He asked after you when I went to see him earlier this morning.

GERT   Oh did he?

HANK   I believe the phrase was, "Did that hussy Gertrude make it another night?"

GERT   Well, what a charmer.

HANK   He also asked me to tell you to call him.

GERT   Oh he did, did he? What, does he need a good ass-whooping?

HANK   God, I hope not.

GERT   Humph. Well, maybe I'll call him, maybe I won't.

HANK   He, uh, texts too.

GERT   Well. You can tell your father that I don't send nudes unless I see the goods first.

HANK   Jesus.

GERT   You make sure you tell him.

HANK   Oh, I'd rather not.

ALEXIS and BEN enter, still wearing their birthday hats.

BEN   Ok, we are ready to celebrate— (Sees HANK) Oh. Huh. Didn't know we were also celebrating Halloween.

FRAN   Oh, good, we have to open your presents.

ALEX   I like the look, Hank. This is for Joe, right Mom?

FRAN   Yes. Do you like it?

ALEX   I do. I think I like it more than Jean Antonik's dress from last year's Drag King Con.

FRAN   That wasn't even my best work.

HANK   Do you exclusively dress Drag Queens, then?

FRAN   I do a little of everything. But those Queens pay well. They always want the highest quality materials. And it can take a lot of yardage.

ALEX   Jean Antonik is six foot seven in platforms.

GERT   Takes a lot of sequins to cover that much Queen.

FRAN   Amen to that. Now, I think you are all set.

HANK   Well, I think I might get changed. As well as this gown does seem to fit in with the New Years theme.

FRAN   (Gasp) Oh my God, what time is it?

BEN   11:59.

FRAN   Oh my gosh, we need to count down.

BEN   Count down?

FRAN   (frantically pouring out the juice into champagne glasses, passing them out to all) Yes! It's almost midnight!

ALEX   You mean it's almost noon.

FRAN   Same difference. Only happens twice a day. And I need to trade out the New Years Decorations for Hanukkah.

GERT   We aren't even Jewish.

FRAN   That doesn't mean we can't celebrate.

BEN   Pretty sure that is exactly what that means.

FRAN   Ok, everyone, take your drink!

HANK   Is this alcohol?

GERT   God, I wish it were, Hank.

FRAN   (Presses a button on her phone, and Auld Lange Sine
        starts to play.) Ok, time to count down. Ben, at 12,
        you get to drop the ball (Hands BEN a rubber ball,
        decorated in sparkles. Pushing ALEXIS to the clock
        she has hanging, moving the hands to almost mid-
        night) And Alexis, you get to move the clock.

ALEX   Is this really necessary?

FRAN   Yes!

GERT   No.

FRAN   Ok, Ten.

GERT   Why.

FRAN   Nine.

GERT   Why can't we be a normal family? (FRAN places a top
        hat on GERT's head)

FRAN   Eight. Come on, guys!

GERT   A family I would be proud to bring boyfriends home
        to.

FRAN   Seven. Mom, you never bring anyone home.

GERT   Can you blame me?

FRAN   Six! Guys, help me count. (Takes up a noisemaker,
        hands one to HANK)

UNISON Five, Four, Three—

At the kitchen door, CARL and SHELLEY appear, and CARL

opens the door and lets them inside.

UNISON   Two—

BEN   Dad!

FRAN   Carl?

ALEX   Shelley!

HANK   What?

GERT   ONE! (She blows the noisemaker and throws her hat into the air. It lands with a thud.) Happy New Year, Bitches!

BLACKOUT

END ACT ONE

ACT 2

SCENE 1

The morning after Shelley and Carl have arrived.

Kitchen. SHELLEY is in the kitchen, making some coffee. ALEX enters, looks glad to see SHELLEY.

ALEX   Good morning. You're up early!

SHELLEY Well, good morning. I always have been an early ris-
               er, since I was a little girl. Had to get up early to take
               care of the chickens and the horses. What about you?
               What's your reason for being up so early?

ALEX   Well, to be honest, I didn't get much sleep. I was wor-
               ried about Mom. She seemed a little on edge after yes-
               terday's debacle.

SHELLEY Debacle? Oh, you mean on account of Carl and I ar-
               riving earlier than expected, and seeing your Mom's
               drag queen friend all made up, and your grandmother
               shouting Happy New Year, Bitches. That sure was a
               hoot and a half.

ALEX   I think Dad was a little less amused by it all.

SHELLEY Oh, you know your Dad. He is not a fan of surprises.

ALEX   I guess he and Mom did have that in common.

FRAN enters, carrying a box of decorations.

FRAN   Good Morning, sweetie. Oh, good morning, Mi-
               chelle. Shelley. Shel? I don't know which you prefer.

SHEL Any of the above.

FRAN Oh, ok. Shel. Michelle. Shelley.

SHEL Or all of the above, I suppose.

FRAN Right. Just Shelley.

SHEL I just wanted to apologize for arriving so unexpect-edly. (Passes Fran a coffee) I was just so anxious to be here, and meet you all, Carl drove through the night.

FRAN You wanted to meet me?

SHEL Well of course I did, silly.

FRAN Oh. That's kind of sweet.

SHEL I have a feeling all of Carl's good traits are on account of you.

FRAN Wow. You are really hard to dislike. Maybe it's your accent.

SHEL Could be.

FRAN Thanks for making coffee. I have to say, I could use one this morning.

ALEX Do you need a shot of bourbon in it?

FRAN We'll see how the rest of the morning goes.

SHEL Your drag queen friend left so quick yesterday, I didn't get a chance to meet them.

FRAN Oh, Hank's not a drag queen. He's my handyman. Er. My tenant, too.

SHEL Ah, a renaissance man. I see.

FRAN   I guess you could say that.

ALEX   Mom made that dress for a client.

SHEL   Oh my goodness gracious, you made that dress?

FRAN   I did.

SHEL   I absolutely loved it!

FRAN   Really?

SHEL   Oh, you betcha!

FRAN   Well, thank you.

SHEL   I wore one almost exactly the same for the Miss Minnesota Pageant. Darlene ended up taking first, but I was second runner up. Although, mine had smaller shoulders.

FRAN   And it probably wasn't a tear away dress.

SHEL   I don't think so.

HANK knocks at the kitchen door.

FRAN   Ah, speak of the drag queen and she shall appear.

HANK   Sorry to bother you ladies this morning.

FRAN   Not a problem. Never a problem. Well, I guess it could be a problem if we were busy or something. Or nude. But we're not. So... no problem.

HANK   Right. Is Gertrude around? Told her I'd drive her to the nursing home today.

FRAN   Provided she didn't sneak out when I wasn't looking. I'll go get her.

FRAN leaves.

SHEL   I didn't introduce myself yesterday, so rude of me.

HANK   I did kind of make myself scarce. Tried not to make a scene.

ALEX   Hard to not make a scene in a show stopping gown like that.

HANK   Not exactly subtle, huh?

SHEL   Well, I'm Shelley Nelson-Olson.

HANK   Nelson-Olson. Are you from the Dakotas?

SHEL   Minnesota. America's heart. Where are you from?

HANK   Jersey. America's armpit.

ALEX   You said you're taking Grandma to the nursing home?

HANK   Yeah. I am headed to see my Dad. She asked if I could give her a lift. Didn't say who she was visiting.

ALEX   Probably every eligible man over the age of sixty.

FRAN reappears with GERT.

FRAN   Found her trying to climb out the upstairs window.

GERT   Can you blame me? The tension in this house since last night has been thick as pea soup. I don't cope well with awkwardness.

ALEX   I'm surprised you haven't jumped out the window before now, in that case.

GERT   The thought's occurred. Hank, you look slightly less fabulous than you did yesterday.

HANK   To be honest, I feel less fabulous.

GERT   Do I sense a career change in your future?

HANK   If only I could dance.

GERT   Pity. I think I hear the boys coming down the stairs. We should peace out before things get weirder here.

HANK   Weirder?

FRAN   It's not going to get weird.

GERT   What're today's holidays?

FRAN   It's Halloween Independence Day.

GERT   (To Hank) You can't make this shit up. Now, come on Hank. Let's blow this pop stand. (HANK gives a little wave as they exit)

FRAN   I think those holidays go perfectly together. (She starts going through her box of décor, pulling out a few pumpkins) Alexis, help me decorate?

ALEX   Sure. (Grabbing some flag garlands.) Nope, not weird at all.

CARL and BEN enter, chummy.

FRAN   Ben, this is one of the first times you've been up before eleven in a long time.

CARL   Benny and I are going to head to the batting cages. He wanted to get an early start. Alexis, you want to come with us?

ALEX   I think I'll stick here. Shelley and I were going to go shopping.

SHEL   A little bonding, just us girls.

FRAN looks between them.

FRAN   You're all leaving?

ALEX   Well, Mom, Shelley and I were going to ask you to come with us.

FRAN   Oh, I see.

CARL   You ok, Francine?

FRAN   Well, today was supposed to be Halloween Independence Day.

BEN   We can celebrate a little later, when we get back.

FRAN   I suppose so.

ALEX   It'll be better to do at night, so we can trick-or-treat and then watch the fireworks you got.

CARL   You have pyrotechnics? Is that wise?

BEN   Dad, it's not Fourth of July without fireworks.

CARL   It's the end of August. What is going on? And Halloween at this time of year?

FRAN   We are just getting in all the holidays before the kids leave.

CARL   This was your idea, Francine?

FRAN   Of course.

CARL   I should have known, I guess.

FRAN   What is that supposed to mean?

CARL   It's just a classic Francine idea, that's all.

FRAN   You don't have to participate, obviously.

SHEL   I think it sounds super fun!

FRAN   Thank you, Shelley.

CARL   Maybe you really should get out the house for today, Francine.

FRAN   I'm not crazy, Carl. I just want the chance to enjoy time with Alexis and Ben before they leave for the year. I figured you would understand. Then again, you have only seen them for one holiday out of the year since you moved across the country. Have fun today, you all. (Exits, juggling an armful of pumpkins and flags and witch hats.)

CARL   What is going on in this house? Do you kids seriously enjoy all this craziness?

BEN   It's not craziness. Like you said, it's classic Mom.

ALEX   And it's been fun. Granted, it's a bit unorthodox...

BEN   But we are kind of an unorthodox family anyway.

ALEX   And besides, at least we are getting to spend time with mom doing stuff. It would be more of a bummer if we just moped around the house.

CARL   (Sighs) I guess I shouldn't have expected anything less from your Mother.

ALEX   You don't have to say it like it's a bad thing, Dad.

SHEL   I for one am excited to celebrate Halloween and Fourth of July. I love costumes and America.

BEN   See, Dad? It'll be a good time.

ALEX   We can pick out Halloween costumes when we are out shopping, Shelley.

SHEL   Oh, perfect! They will probably be on super clearance. I'll make sure to get you a great costume, Carl. (Gives him a peck on the cheek)

CARL   I still think this is all a little whacko.

BEN   It'll be fun. I am going to grab my bat, Dad, then we can head to the batting cages. (BEN exits)

ALEX   Come on, Shelley. We can look through my old costume trunk and see what I might have already for tonight.

As SHELLEY and ALEXIS exit, they squeeze past FRAN as she enters again.

FRAN   Off to shop?

SHEL   Off to find costumes for tonight! (EXIT)

FRAN   (Awkwardly turning to CARL. They are alone, for the first time in years) Alexis seems to really like Shelley, huh? They are thick as thieves.

CARL   I think it's nice, don't you?

FRAN   I think it makes sense. There is probably only a few years' age difference between them.

CARL   (Sarcastically) Funny.

FRAN   But true.

CARL   What about that Hank guy? The one in the dress?

FRAN   What about him?

CARL   Ben said he lives here?

FRAN   He just lives on top of me. Er, rather, on top of the garage. Over the garage. He's my tenant. I am renting it out to him. Well, not renting. We bartered. He is fixing things for me, and I let him live there.

CARL   Is that safe?

FRAN   For me. I don't know how safe it is for him. Things keep breaking up there. All that duct taping you did.

CARL   Well, I am sorry I am not a handy man.

FRAN   It's fine, he's filling up all the holes you left. Well, you know what I mean.

CARL   So are you dating him?

FRAN   Dating him? What? No. Like I said, he's my tenant who lives on top of me. Above me. Above the garage.

CARL   You seem like you like him.

FRAN   Why do you say that?

CARL   Well, you used to like me, and you got all tongue tied like that when we were younger, and still together.

FRAN   It's not that I don't like you anymore, Carl. I like you just fine. I even still love you a little. Not like that, but the same way you can love how you looked in an old pair of jeans, but you like how you look better now that you've lost weight and grown out of them.

CARL   What?

FRAN   It took you leaving me to realize that you didn't fit anymore with who I had become. And that's ok.

CARL   Yeah. Look, Francine. You've... you've done a great job with our kids. I love you for that.

FRAN   Thanks, Carl.

CARL   And if this whole holiday thing makes it easier for you to see them go, then I guess you have to do what you have to do. We'll be back later, so if you want to have this little celebration thing, we can do that.

FRAN   Good. Have fun with Ben.

CARL   I hope you decide to go out with Shelley and Alexis. I think you'll actually get along with Shelley.

FRAN   But she's two decades younger than me. What will we talk about?

CARL   I am sure you have a lot in common. With her Nana. (Smiles, exits).

FRAN   (Thinks for a minute, then goes to the door. Calling off) Alexis? Shelley? I think I will go shopping with you both today after all!

SCENE 2

Halloween Independence Day dinner.

FRAN, GERT, ALEX, BEN, SHELLEY, and CARL are all sitting around, pumpkins of candy and American flags in front of them. FRAN is dressed as a witch, ALEX is dressed as Wonder Woman, BEN as a baseball player, Carl as a vampire, and SHELLEY as a princess. GERT is wearing a skintight, skimpy cat costume. They are all sorting their candy, talking about their days.

BEN   And then Dad winds up and just does this spectacu-
         lar swing... and the ball floats up at the last minute...

CARL   And it whacked me right in the shoulder. I couldn't
         believe it.

FRAN   Your depth perception really has gone, hasn't it?

CARL   Give me a high five, and we will find out. (They try,
         and he misses by a lot) Yeah, it's pretty bad.

BEN   And while we there, we saw Chrissy Kline, Alexis.

ALEX   Did you talk to her?

BEN   Are you kidding? She hated me in high school.

ALEX   You always had such a huge crush on her.

BEN   I wasn't the only one.

ALEX   So you didn't even say hi?

CARL   He chickened out.

ALEX & GERT   Wuss.

BEN   Grandma! You aren't supposed to gang up on me.

GERT   But you were being a wuss.

FRAN   Actually, speaking of dates. Alexis, you never told me how your date the other night went?

ALEX   Oh. Um. Not great.

FRAN   No? I thought you were excited about it?

SHEL   Alex said her date didn't even offer to pay. And smelled like Doritos.

FRAN   Oh. You didn't tell me that.

ALEX   Yeah, well, Shelley and I were talking about it when we were trying on clothes and stuff today. You were at the Candle store.

FRAN   I did get some nice new candles. The two we have here on the table are called "Harvest Pumpkin" and "Red, White, and Blue".

GERT   Not sure you are supposed to burn them together.

FRAN   I wish you would've told me your date didn't go well. I would have found that boy and scolded him for being rude to my girl.

ALEX   Shelley already helped me write the perfect rejection text to send, so it's all good.

FRAN   Oh.

ALEX   Just, you know, not my type.

GERT   What is your type?

ALEX   I don't know....

BEN	Blonde. A cool accent, right, Alex?
SHEL	Oh, I guess it's good you are going to be in Scotland, then. Plenty of fun accents there!
CARL	Just don't go getting married and moving there permanently.
FRAN	That's just what I said!
BEN	Speaking of traveling. Dad, I was thinking we should try to take a detour on our way to Cali. Maybe we can stop in Colorado, and I can visit some of my friends for a few nights.
CARL	I don't see why not.
FRAN	Well, you won't have time. You have to get back to California to make it there for your first day of classes. Right?
BEN	Oh. Yeah.
CARL	Ben, don't you think you should tell her?
FRAN	Tell me what?
BEN	Nothing.
FRAN	Nothing?
CARL	Ben?
FRAN	Is there something I'm missing, here?
BEN	Classes, uh. I talked to my professors and they said because I am driving there, it's ok that I will miss the first few days.
FRAN	Really? That sounds strange. I can't believe they were ok with that. I would still try to get there before they

start.

BEN   Right. Well, yeah, we can see.

FRAN   You knew about it, Carl? And didn't want to let me in on it?

CARL   I knew. Yeah.

FRAN   I guess I am just out of the loop on everything. Mom, anything you want to share with the class? You were gone for most of the day, and you haven't said anything yet about any randy old men you met today.

GERT   Slow day.

FRAN   That's it?

GERT   I don't wanna talk about it.

FRAN   Sounds like a theme here, tonight.

HANK knocks on the door, lets himself in.

HANK   Uh, hi all. Didn't mean to interrupt.

FRAN   No, it's ok, Hank. Everyone was just busy not telling me anything.

HANK   Right. Well, I am just going to take a look at the ice maker in your fridge. You said it's not working?

FRAN   It's just letting out little drips of water at a time.

GERT   It's got prostate problems.

HANK   Don't we all. I'll take a look. Oh, and by the way, Gertrude. My dad told me to give you this. (Pulls out a letter, passes it to her. Then he starts work on the fridge)

GERT   (Takes it, looking excited) Ahem, 'scuse me, everyone. Feel free to start dinner without me. (Scurries out of the room)

CARL   Speaking of dinner. Francine, I am going to take the kids and Shelley out tomorrow night for dinner. Hope that's ok.

FRAN   Take them out?

CARL   Yeah, I wanted to take them to Firenze for some good Italian food.

FRAN   Don't you like my cooking?

CARL   Oh of course.

SHELLEY   We just don't want to put you out, and make you keep cooking for us.

FRAN   I don't mind.

CARL   The kids mentioned they wanted to go out and do dinner with me and Shel.

FRAN   Oh. I didn't realize.

ALEX   We just haven't gotten a chance to go out with them yet.

BEN   Is that ok, Mom?

CARL   I mean, you could come if you wanted to, I suppose.

FRAN   No, it seems like I won't be wanted there.

SHEL   That's nonsense. Of course you'd be wanted.

CARL   I just figured you might also like a night off. You know, to yourself. Empty house, that type of thing.

FRAN   What am I supposed to do by myself?

CARL   Well, for one thing, you can take a break from celebrating a holiday tomorrow.

FRAN   But tomorrow was going to be Valentine's Day. I was going to make heart shaped cakes.

ALEX   We don't have to go out, Mom.

FRAN   No, no. I don't want to be a party pooper. You should all go out tomorrow night. Have some dinner at Firenze. I'll be fine here by myself.

BEN   You sure?

FRAN   Oh, of course.

HANK   (Clearing his throat, chiming in.) Looks like there's a part in the ice maker that's broken. I can get it at the hardware store tomorrow.

FRAN   That's fine. Thanks, Hank.

HANK   Happy Halloween Fourth of July, everyone. (He exits)

FRAN   I think... I think I will head to bed, now. I'm getting a little tired. I'll... I'll see you all in the morning. If anyone is around, I can make heart-shaped pancakes. (Fran exits, removing her witches hat as she goes.)

ALEX   I think you hurt her feelings, Dad.

CARL   No, I didn't. You heard her, she's tired.

BEN   We should try to convince her to come tomorrow.

CARL   I thought you both said you wanted time together with me and Shelley?

ALEX   Well, yeah, but...

CARL   It'll be fun. Come on, why don't we go watch a movie.

BEN   I think Mom had The Shining cued up for us, followed by Independence Day.

CARL   What a double feature.

SHEL   Oh, that might give me nightmares.

ALEX   We can always do something else if you get freaked out, Shelley.

SHEL   Oh, you are such a sweetpea. Come on, you'll sit next to me.

They all exit out of the kitchen, blackout.

SCENE 3

Later that night.

SHELLEY comes into the kitchen, finds ALEXIS is already there, starting to put up decorations for Valentine's Day for her Mom.

SHEL   You're still up?

ALEX   Oh, you scared me.

SHEL   Not as much as The Shining scared me. Those twins were spooky.

ALEX   Ben and I dressed up as them for Halloween last year. It was a good gag.

SHEL   Speaking of Halloween... Does this (gestures to decorations) mean that Halloween Fourth is over?

ALEX   Yeah, I guess so. I just wanted to put these up for my Mom. She seemed pretty down, I am hoping when she wakes up and sees these, it'll make her smile.

SHEL   Aren't you just the sweetest thing, doing that for her.

ALEX   Well, if we can't be together tomorrow night for Valentine's Dinner, we can at least have a pink and red and heart-decked morning.

SHEL   Let me help.

ALEX   Thanks. (Glances over at SHELLEY as they decorate together) You know, you've been surprisingly cool about all of this.

SHEL   All of what? You mean the holiday celebration stuff?

Or the staying in my boyfriend's ex-wife's house?

ALEX   Both. It's weird to hear you call him your boyfriend. He seems so... old to be called that.

SHEL   Sometimes I'll tell the girls at work that he's my significant other. Sounds a little more mature.

ALEX   I don't actually know where you work. Is it at a salon?

SHEL   Actually, I work in Human Resources at a Law Firm.

ALEX   Oh, wow. I didn't expect that.

SHEL   Because I seem more the cosmetology type?

ALEX   Well, you do always look like you just came from a spa. I'm sorry if I assumed.

SHEL   I like to look my best. But I am not insulted or anything that you thought I worked at a salon. Everyone is good at something. I stink at painting nails, and the one time I tried to dye my hair it turned purple. So I leave it to the professionals.

ALEX   Do you like working in Law?

SHEL   I do like where I am at. But there is something that's holding me back, I think.

ALEX   Really?

SHEL   Yes. I kind of have a sense that there's something that's holding you back, too. Something you haven't told anyone. A secret.

ALEX   A secret? Me? No.

SHEL   Alex, we've been spending lots of time together since I got here. I picked up on it right away.

ALEX	You did? Do you think anyone else knows?
SHEL	No. But you can always feel ok telling me.
ALEX	But, then it's not a secret anymore.
SHEL	I promise I won't tell anyone.
ALEX	Well....
SHEL	You know, everyone has secrets. Even me. But even a little itsy bitsy secret can eat you up inside if you keep it to yourself too long. (She wraps an arm around ALEX's shoulder.) If you think it'll make you feel better, you can trust me with your secret.
ALEX	(Looks up at SHELLEY for a long moment, then swiftly leans in to kiss SHELLEY)
SHEL	(Stepping away, holding up her hands) Oopsie. Um, I think you may have misunderstood.
ALEX	Your... your secret isn't that you have a crush on me too?
SHEL	Oh Heavens to Betsy, no.
ALEX	Oh, God. I'm so embarrassed. I thought you were saying...
SHEL	Don't be embarrassed, Sweetpea. I am so flattered that you feel that way about me. But I'm afraid I am a fan of the man parts.
ALEX	Oh, no. I'm sorry.
SHEL	Never apologize for who you are, Alexis. Now, why don't you say it aloud. Who are you?
ALEX	(Letting out a long sigh) I am... gay.

SHEL	See, doesn't it feel better to say it out loud?
ALEX	I still can't stop feeling embarrassed. I have a crush on my Dad's girlfriend. Ew.
SHEL	Wouldn't be the first person in that situation. Think about that boy in the song Stacey's Mom.
ALEX	Not quite the same.
SHEL	Ok, fair.
ALEX	And you knew?
SHEL	I guessed. You flirt a little better than your Mom does with that handyman.
ALEX	Thank God for that.
SHEL	I am just surprised you haven't told anyone yet.
ALEX	Well, Ben knows. He caught me stealing the Victoria's Secret catalogues back from his room, and he knows I don't buy any of that stuff. He was cool about it.
SHEL	Don't you think your Mom and Dad would be ok with it?
ALEX	I don't know. It's hard to tell. And honestly, I am really nervous about it.
SHEL	But you told me, and it wasn't so bad, was it? Aside from the lip-locking incident.
ALEX	Don't remind me.
SHEL	You trusted me. Don't you think you can trust your Mom?
ALEX	I trusted you because I thought maybe you liked me too.

SHEL   I do like you. And I care for you. But not that way. Maybe you like me because you trust me, not trust me because you like me.

ALEX   Yeah. It's a lot of confusing feelings all at once. I just know that I never got the appeal of Chris Hemsworth, but I go gaga for Scarlett Johansson.

SHEL   Well, ok, that I can understand.

ALEX   The thing is... It's not that I think my mom would disown me or anything. But I don't want to disappoint her. You know what I mean? I am her only daughter, I am her baby, at least by a few minutes. She always talks about how I will probably meet and marry a handsome Scotsman, or how I have to bring home more boyfriends to the house. Or she talks about how she can't wait for me to have babies. Or how I was always her little princess, and how I always will be. I don't want to tarnish that for her. I don't want her to ever look at me and feel sad about who I love. I want her to still share things with me, and still treat me the way she always has. I am just scared something will change when I tell her. And with me going away, we are already not going to be able to talk every day. What if she stops asking about my life, or stops worrying about me? She's my Mom. I want to be able to tell her when I meet a girl I like, or bring someone home to meet her. I'm not worried that she would kick me out of the house. I'm just worried I won't feel as welcomed coming back.

SHEL   (Wrapping ALEX up in a hug) Firstly, you could never disappoint your mother. She loves you, unconditionally. When my own Mama found out I was dating a man almost thirty years older than me, she was surprised. She might have been unsure. But once she saw how happy I was, she let it be, and learned to be happy for me. Secondly, your Mom's visions of who you are will certainly change when you tell her, and things may be different for a while. But one thing you can't change is your feelings. And so when you come home to visit with your tall, beautiful Scottish girlfriend, your Mom will see you being your true self. And so she will see her little princess happy, and it will make her happy.

ALEX   (Letting out a little laugh, a smile) Thank you, Shelley. You are too good at being a stepmother already.

SHEL   Well, I plan to be in your lives. I want to make sure they are good ones.

ALEX   You said you had a secret, too. What is it?

SHEL   Oh, well.

ALEX   I told you a big secret. You owe me one.

SHEL   I guess I could tell you. But you can't tell anyone else. Deal?

ALEX   (Gasp) Am I going to be a big sister?

SHEL   No! You know, I knew I shouldn't have worn that high-waisted dress. It always makes me look bigger than I am.

ALEX   So what is the secret?

SHEL   I had been toying with the idea of going to Law School. And last week I got my acceptance letter for the spring term at Harvard.

ALEX   Whoa!

SHEL	I know. I didn't really expect to get in. But they wanted me.
ALEX	That's great!
SHEL	Well, except for one thing.
ALEX	What?
SHEL	Harvard's on the East Coast, and your Dad is on the West Coast.
ALEX	Well, what did he say when you told him?

SHELLEY hems and haws.

ALEX	You didn't tell him?
SHEL	I didn't even tell him I applied.
ALEX	Why not?
SIIEL	I thought it might mean that he'd break things off with me.
ALEX	And you don't want him to?
SHEL	Of course not. I may not be the same age as your father, but we have a lot in common. I'm an old soul, always have been.
ALEX	Would you have Dad move to Boston with you?
SHEL	I can't take him away from his work. I think we can make long-distance work. I mean, this is my career, my future! I like to think he would do whatever it takes to help me achieve my dream. I don't want to lose him. But if he doesn't want to emotionally support me furthering my career, then I worry what might happen.

ALEX   That is a big secret.

SHEL   I guess we both have things to tell your Mom and Dad.

ALEX   I think we both need to sleep on it, to decide how to do this.

SHEL   I agree.

ALEX   Let's make a deal. Before leaving Mom's house, we both have to come clean.

SHEL   I don't want to push you out of the closet, Sweetpea.

ALEX   I think I am ready to come out of it.

SHEL   In that case...You have yourself a deal. But I may wait until after our Valentine's Day dinner. If I say anything before appetizers, things might get weird.

ALEX   Oh, that's fair. I do hope Mom will be ok by herself at home tomorrow night.

SHEL   I hope so too. Does she have any hobbies, something we can convince her to do tomorrow while we are gone?

ALEX   I don't really think she has any hobbies.

SHEL   She must have something she does in her down time.

ALEX   She never has down time. Between working and raising us, it was a handful. You know what's strange? For so long I have just thought of her as a mom, like that was her main role. It's pretty selfish of me.

SHEL   I think she just needs to remember what it was like to be Francine, not Mom.

ALEX   She does love music. Maybe I'll make her a playlist to listen to while we are out tomorrow. All her favorites from when she was younger. Kind of remind her what it used to be like.

SHEL   I think that's a great idea.

ALEX   Speaking of hobbies… there is one thing I wanted to ask you.

SHEL   What's that?

ALEX   You said you were almost crowned Miss Minnesota.

SHEL   Second runner up.

ALEX   What was your talent for the pageant?

SHEL   Oh, well. I didn't want to put all my eggs in one basket. So I danced and sang a Weezer song and played ukulele simultaneously.

ALEX   All at once?

SHEL   I will be the first to admit I might have been overambitious.

ALEX   I don't know. You must have done something right to be runner up.

SHEL   What I mean is, I should have just stuck to those three things. But I also had a flaming hula hoop that I used at the same time.

ALEX   Oh.

SHEL   Things could have gone better.

ALEX   What happened?

SHEL   I caught my dress on fire a teensy bit.

ALEX   What?

SHEL   I kept singing and dancing, though. I am a consummate performer.

ALEX   Despite all that, the other girl still got first? What was her talent? Did she regurgitate a kitten?

SHEL   She played the steel drums on roller blades. Very avant-garde for Minnesota. Plus, her Dad was a season ticket holder for the Vikings. I think she might have greased some palms.

ALEX   How scandalous.

SHEL   Her dress might have gotten a little scorched on my way past her after my act.

ALEX   And was that by mistake, or on purpose?

SHEL   Well... Since I am working toward my law degree... I'll plead the fifth on that one.

BOTH EXIT, Laughing.

SCENE 4

Valentine's Night.

FRAN sits at the dining table, surrounded by sad Valentine's décor and a large, mostly empty bottle of red wine. There is a half-eaten cake on the table. Her iPhone is playing typical sappy romance songs. FRAN starts to lift the wine bottle to pour herself another glass, but she looks between the glass and the bottle. Then she shrugs and takes a swig of the wine straight out of the bottle. She wipes her mouth with one of the heart-shaped decorations on the table. She shoves a forkful of cake in her mouth, and makes a sound of contentment.

FRAN then shakily stands up from the table, taking the wine and her fork with her. She pokes at the phone, until an upbeat 80's ballad comes on. She lets out a sound of excited recognition, then starts to sway to the song. Then she begins to lip-sync into the fork. Then she starts fully dancing, getting into the song and not noticing as HANK comes to the door, knocking. She still doesn't see him enter, watching her with a smile.

During her dance finale, she finally turns and spots HANK. She lets out a yelp, and almost drops her wine. HANK steps forward and grabs it, standing close to her.

HANK   That was close. Sorry, I didn't mean to scare you.

FRAN   (Tipsy) You didn't scare me. Not too bad, I mean. You just popped up. (Wagging her fork) You are lucky I'm not armed. I might have thought you were an intruder.

HANK   I did knock.

FRAN   I didn't hear it.

HANK   So I let myself in.

FRAN   I was having myself a little dance party.

FRAN Turns off the music, after several attempted pokes at her
         phone.

HANK   I noticed.

FRAN   Did you like it?

HANK   It was something to behold.

FRAN   Thank you.

HANK   Not necessarily a compliment.

FRAN   You liked it.

HANK   Having a good evening, are you?

FRAN   Well, everyone left me here.

HANK   I know. I heard.

FRAN   Carl and Shelley took the kids out to dinner. They
         kept saying I was invited. But I could tell they didn't
         really want me. So I said no, no, I would invite some
         friends over and have cake and wine. And then after
         they left I remembered for the past eighteen years, my
         kids have been my life. And I don't have that many
         friends.

HANK   I am sure you have friends, Francine.

FRAN   No, I don't. Even my mail delivery lady Bethany
         doesn't know my name, even though I always give her
         a soda on her way through. My own mail lady doesn't
         know my name. My name is on every single piece of

mail she delivers, Hank.

HANK   You must have some people you consider your friends.

FRAN   I used to have so many friends. But Carl got them all in the divorce. I mean, I have a few close friends. But they are all happily married, and it would be sad if I was a third wheel. Or a fifth wheel. Or a seventh wheel. Or a... (Tries to count on her fingers) Another wheel, you know.

HANK   I get it. My wife got most of my friends in the divorce too.

FRAN   You get it, Hank. You're so nice to me. I don't know why.

HANK   You do have the power to evict me.

FRAN   Oh, I would never do that.

HANK   That's not why I'm nice to you. It's because I like you as a person.

FRAN   Oh.

HANK   I mean, you're an odd duck. But I like that. You make me smile.

FRAN   Glad I can be of assistance.

HANK   So you were saying that everyone left.

FRAN   Was I?

HANK   You were.

FRAN   I forgot. Oh, yeah. Everyone left. They all went out to dinner. Even my Mom is being secretive. She said she had things to do. Things, Hank. She said she had things to do. Not men to do. Things. And she got all defensive when I tried to tease her about who her flavor of the week is. (Leaning in conspiratorially) She asked my opinion on her outfit.

HANK   She doesn't usually?

FRAN   Never. She actually called me into her room, just like when I was a kid. When she used to try on outfits and have me pick which one she should wear for her dates with my Dad. They were married for forty-five years, and they still went on a date every week. So tonight, she did her hair the way she used to. She wore a brooch that was my favorite when I was little. And she actually asked me if her dress looked nice. Nice, not tight, not boobalicious. Nice.

HANK   That's good, isn't it?

FRAN   It's weird. After my Dad died, she started in on her slutty phase. Pardon my French. I don't like that word. But she is going through a slutty phase. But tonight, she seemed all giddy, just like she did before dates with my dad. I don't know what's gotten into her.

HANK   So your Mom went out, too?

FRAN   Yep. So here I was, with a whole cake and a whole bottle of wine, and no friends. At least Alex made me this nice playlist. She said she remembered how I used to tell her stories of me wanting to be on Dance Fever when I was younger. It was so sweet of her to remember. Do you want some wine? I'm so rude, I'm sorry.

HANK   I saw a lot of your backwash go into that wine bottle. I think I'll take a rain- check.

FRAN   There's beer in the fridge.

HANK   You haven't already chugged that?

FRAN   The night's still young.

HANK   (Going to the fridge, grabbing a beer) I'm sorry you got abandoned tonight.

FRAN   I mean, I can't say I blame them. I am kind of a wreck. Look at this place. Decorations everywhere. What kind of psycho am I, inflicting all of this cheesy crap on my kids? It's crazy, isn't it?

HANK   It may be a little crazy. But it comes from a place of love.

FRAN   I do love my kids. I love them so much. I don't want to lose them. They are going to be on opposite sides of the world from me. I need to remind them of all the good times we have had. Otherwise. Otherwise they may never choose to come back. When children move out, usually they come to see their parents for the holidays. At first. At first, you see them for every little thing. They come home to do laundry, to get home-cooked food, to be with their parents at every break, every Monday holiday, on Labor Day or Memorial Day. But then before long the drive gets too long. They have plans on holiday weekends. They have families of their own. And before you know it, you only see them every other Thanksgiving. I wanted to remind Alexis and Ben how much fun we can have, even on the stupid holidays. So they will come back to see me, even if the drive is long, or if they have their own washing machine, or if they move to Canada.

HANK   You can tell they love you, too. Who wouldn't want to come home to you?

FRAN   And yet, here I am. Alone. On Valentine's Day. Or whatever.

HANK   Well, you're not completely alone anymore. (Gestures to himself) You looking for a Valentine's Date? You got one.

FRAN   I don't want a pity date.

HANK   It's not a pity date. Because believe it or not, no one invited me out to dinner tonight either. So really, you'd be having pity on me if you ask me out tonight.

FRAN   Really?

HANK   Yes. So, Francine, will you be my Valentine tonight?

FRAN   (Smiling) I would like that.

HANK   Oh, good. In that case, (he goes to the door and reaches outside to grab his tool box) I have something for you.

FRAN   Are you going to fix the electric socket that stopped working?

HANK   Nothing quite so practical, I'm afraid. (He pulls out a bouquet of flowers, a red box of chocolate, and a small teddy bear) Cheesy Valentine's gifts for my Valentine.

FRAN   Oh my goodness. For me?

HANK   I thought it kind of sucky for Carl to steal your kids away from you on Valentine's Day. So I picked these up the way any good Valentine's Date should: in the clearance section of Walmart. Because I knew you might be feeling bummed being alone.

FRAN   I love them. Thank you.

HANK   Would have been really awkward if you said no to being my Valentine.

FRAN   Well, let's cheers to Valentine's dates, then.

FRAN clinks her wine bottle with HANK's beer bottle. HANK walks over and points at FRAN's phone.

HANK   What other tunes did Alex put on here for you?

FRAN   Oh, she picked some good ones.

FRAN crosses to the table, picks up her phone, and starts fiddling with it, skipping through songs.

FRAN   Alexis said Ben helped her find all the best throwbacks. He calls this stuff super retro.

HANK   These are retro? I thought the 1950s were retro. This is the stuff I used to groove to.

FRAN   Me too! I loved dancing. If I had the time I would take it up again. Go take hip hop classes, or join a ballroom dance team.

HANK   With your kids heading out, you may have time for that stuff now.

FRAN   You know what? You're right. I am going to have so much time to finally do all the stuff I was putting off.

HANK   Like take dance classes.

FRAN   Take dance classes. Join a book club for women who love trashy romances. Do that Indian food cooking class downtown. Try to keep some of the plants in my garden alive.

HANK   Sounds like you've got plenty to do.

FRAN   You know what? You are right. I have so many things
        I wanted to do before the kids. Why not try them
        all out now? There's no time like the present. Ex-
        cept when it comes to music. (Fiddles again with her
        phone) Music now has got nothing on the 80s.

FRAN starts to skip a song, but HANK catches her hand.

HANK   Hey, this is a good one. Super retro, as Ben would say.

FRAN   Oh, I loved this song. I once made Carl dance with
        me to this one at Charlene Mitchell's house in Col-
        lege. Her parents were out of town, and Carl got so
        wasted. Halfway through the song he puked spiked
        fruit punch on my white mini skirt.

HANK   Carl's a peach.

FRAN   Come on, let's dance.

HANK   I don't really dance.

FRAN   You saw my moves. You can't possibly be worse than
        I am.

FRAN pulls HANK into a dance. He's reluctant at first, then gets
into it.

HANK   Promise you won't throw up red wine on my white
        mini skirt?

FRAN   That gives me an idea for your next drag outfit.

HANK   Not going to lie, that shit was comfortable. Pardon
        my French.

FRAN   Hey, you are a good dancer.

HANK   I think you have beer goggles on.

FRAN   Nope. I thought you were cute before I drank a bottle of wine.

HANK   Oh ho, so you think I'm cute?

FRAN   I thought you were an exotic dancer when I met you for a reason.

HANK   Oh right, how could I forget.

FRAN   And you thought when you saw me... "This must be Gertrude's older sister", right?

HANK   (Stops dancing, pulls FRAN close to him) No, I thought... (Brushing her hair out of her face) I want to sock whatever jerk made this woman feel anything less than what she is   beautiful. And then I thought, oh, she's a little crazy, isn't she? And funny as hell. It's a killer combination, Francine.

FRAN   You think I'm beautiful?

HANK   Of course I do.

FRAN   No one's called me that in a long time. Not that I put much self-worth on that kind of thing, but when it's been a really long time since someone said that, you start to feel kind of schlumpy. (FRAN moves in closer to FRANK, toying with his shirt collar) I don't even think that's a word. It's more of a feeling. (HANK moves in a little closer, wrapping his arms around her waist) You know what I mean. I mean, maybe you do. Or maybe you don't. In any case, it's nice to hear that you think that, and I think you're beautiful too, in a manly kind of way, and... and can you please stop me from talking?

HANK swoops in and kisses FRAN. After a few moments, they break apart, a little breathless, smiling, awkward.

FRAN   That did it.

HANK   Hope that was ok.

FRAN   Better than ok.

HANK   Been a while.

FRAN   Me too. Gosh, it's been a long while. I mean, not like things are turning to dust or anything, but... I guess I forgot how nice it is to be kissed.

HANK   Glad I could oblige.

FRAN   And confusing. Kisses are confusing. I forgot that too.

HANK   Confusing how? I think you nailed it.

FRAN   No, I mean. The feelings that happen along with them. You know. Overthinking is kind of my specialty. I don't really know what it means. But I know I liked it. If that makes sense.

HANK   I get it. And I feel that too. Look, I know you've got a lot going on with everything. But maybe once things quiet down, would you maybe like to go out to dinner with me? In between dance classes and cooking classes and gardening.

FRAN   Like a date?

HANK   Yeah, a date.

FRAN   That would be nice.

HANK   Great. You can just, you know, tell me when. I'll be around. You know. Upstairs. Above you. Well, above the garage. You know where it is. Your house. You know.

FRAN   Look who's babbling now?

HANK   You got me a little tongue tied. (Glancing toward the door) It's getting kind of late. I guess I'll leave you to it. I am sure you have to prep for tomorrow's holiday.

FRAN   Right. New day, new holiday.

HANK   What are you celebrating tomorrow?

FRAN   Thanksgiving.

HANK   Best holiday of them all. Best food.

FRAN   I like it too. Um, Hank? Would you maybe want to come to Thanksgiving tomorrow?

HANK   I don't want to intrude on your family time.

FRAN   It'd be nice to have you there. Not just to fix a leak or something. But to spend time with us.

HANK   I'd like that. I'll be here.

FRAN   Good. I'll see you tomorrow.

HANK   See you around. (Exits)

FRAN is alone in the kitchen, looking around. Smiling to herself, she sits down at the table. She leans her cheek on her hand, and takes another swig of wine, humming happily to herself.

BLACKOUT

Lights come back up on the same scene still night, but now FRAN is passed out on the table, snoring. CARL enters, goes to the fridge to get a drink, hears the snores and looks over at

FRAN. He walks over to her, and places a gentle hand on her shoulder. She immediately jerks upright and groggily grunts.

FRAN   Happy New Year. What? (Rubbing at her face) What happened?

CARL   Frannie, you fell asleep at the table.

FRAN   Oh dear. Oh. Dear. My head.

CARL   Did you drink all this wine by yourself?

FRAN   I had company. But he didn't help me drink it, no.

CARL   He? Is this a special friend of yours?

FRAN   Hank.

CARL   Your handyman turned tenant?

FRAN   Yeah.

CARL   I see.

FRAN   Don't you judge me, Carl. You aren't allowed to judge me, since you came waltzing in here with your cute little girlfriend.

CARL   I wasn't judging. I... I actually think he seems like a good guy.

FRAN   You do?

CARL   Well, he has to have the patience of a saint to be living around here.

FRAN   You're right about that.

CARL   Frannie, I know these past few days haven't been the easiest on you.

FRAN   You're damn skippy.

CARL   But, but, I really do appreciate you taking us in. I know it's a strange situation, with Shelley here. But you've been so kind to her, so accepting. She really likes you a lot.

FRAN   I wasn't intending to like her, Carl. But she makes it darn near impossible not to like her. She's sweet, she's always worrying about making everyone happy, she's got such a big heart when it comes to the kids.

CARL   Seeing the two of you together, it kind of reminds me of why I like her so much. Because she's like you.

FRAN   Like me? I hate to break it to you, Carl, but you and I didn't exactly turn out well.

CARL   No, I know. But she reminds me of you when we were first together, Your passion, your eagerness, your smarts. The you before I dimmed your light.

FRAN   You didn't dim my light.

CARL   I did, though. At first, we were growing up together. Then when we had the kids so young, I got scared, I guess. You always loved the idea of having a family, growing old together, settling in. I decided I didn't want to grow up, and just stopped. I reverted to being a kid myself. And left you alone a lot with the kids. It was a shitty thing to do to you.

FRAN   Normally I would try to argue, and say no, no, it was me, not you. But I am still kind of drunk, and all my politeness has gone out the window. You wanted to be the kids' friend, not their dad. I had to be the bad guy, and because of it you got to be the savior. It sucked. But you know what? I got stronger. I got braver. And

I wasn't alone, I had them. You and I stayed together for them, and you learned to be a better parent to our kids. And we have two pretty good ones.

CARL   You're right. That's mostly thanks to you.

FRAN   I know. And it's funny, Carl. But I see some of myself in Shelley too. But not the old me. I see the new me. The stronger one. She won't let you dim that light of hers, because she shines far too bright. I just hope you know what a good thing you have.

CARL   I do. I am going to try not to mess this up.

FRAN   Good. Because if you break up, I'm keeping her.

CARL   Deal. Now, come on. Might be time for bed, huh? (Standing up from the table, helping FRAN up from the table, starting to cross to the door.)

FRAN   Bed. Yes. Is it possible to be both drunk and hung-over at the same time?

CARL   Oh yeah. You need some sleep.

FRAN   But, tomorrow's Thanksgiving. I know I have things to do. I just can't remember what they are. Carl, in the morning, tell the kids to start the turkey, per my instructions on the counter. And the veggies need to be diced. Small pieces, but not too small otherwise they will burn. And the potato masher works better than the food processor.

CARL   I'll see if I can't wrangle those good kids of ours to do some of that stuff. As for you, you should rest. Maybe sleep in.

FRAN   Sleep in? I never sleep in. Although I guess there's a first time for everything. (Both Exit)

SCENE 5

Thanksgiving Day. Sort of.

The light is rising outside, and SHELLEY and ALEXIS are behind the counter, mashing potatoes and cutting vegetables. BEN is putting a pie in the oven. Carl is hanging a Happy Thanksgiving sign on the door. GERT is setting the table. FRAN suddenly enters, looking disoriented and frazzled.

FRAN   Oh my goodness gracious. I slept in. I never sleep in. Oof, my head. Where is the turkey? Oh, no. We won't be able to have turkey until midnight at this rate. Oh, dear.

BEN and ALEXIS come around and each wrap an arm around FRAN.

BEN   Mom, chill. It's all good.

ALEX   We got the turkey started already, and we've been getting everything ready.

CARL   I even got some decorations.

SHELLEY   I followed your instructions to a T and the pies are baking.

GERT   I even dressed up for the occasion. (GERT shows off a turkey sweater) Not really my style. Too cheesy. It's from your closet. But I did it for you.

FRAN   Oh. Oh, wow. You guys really did do a good job. But... why? I thought this stuff was maybe getting on your nerves.

BEN   We, um, we missed you last night, Mom.

ALEX   Dinner was strange without you. Without a theme.

SHELLEY We wanted to make it up to you this morning, let you sleep in. (Glancing at CARL) We heard you had a wild night.

FRAN   Wild? Me?

BEN   A whole bottle of wine, Mom?

FRAN   It was only most of a bottle.

CARL   Last time I saw you that drunk was the night of our wedding.

BEN   You got wasted at your own wedding?

FRAN   Well, we did get married in Vegas.

ALEX   Vegas? You? How did I not know that?

CARL   We had a real wedding a few months after that. But that was one of the few times your mother was impulsive, I think. She drank me under the table that night. She carried me to bed.

FRAN   I thought what happens in Vegas stays there.

GERT   In this case, what happened in Vegas followed you home. His name is Carl.

FRAN   Anyway, that is a story for another time. Today, it's Thanksgiving, right?

HANK   (Entering through the kitchen) Good afternoon. Hope I'm not late.

FRAN   It's afternoon already?

HANK   I see the wine hit you hard.

FRAN   Sorry, I am not a very good hostess today.

HANK   I brought a side dish.

CARL   Good to see you, Hank. (Shake hands)

GERT   What'd you bring?

HANK   (Showing them off) I thought I'd... turnip.

FRAN   (Cracks up at this) Turnip! Like turn up! Oh, I get it. That's so good.

GERT   I don't know what's worse, Hank. Your pun or the fact that Francine felt the need to explain it.

HANK   I'd say they are both on par.

FRAN   Mom, leave him be. I'll take these. Turnip. Classic Thanksgiving joke.

BEN   Hank, you're joining dinner?

HANK   Hope that's alright. Your Mom invited me.

BEN   Yeah, I think it's awesome. Just beware. Our other Thanksgiving tradition is playing a very intense game of Scrabble after dinner.

HANK   I didn't know Scrabble could be intense.

BEN   Oh, you'll see. Mom's claws come out.

FRAN   Let's, um, have a seat at the table. While we wait for the rest to finish cooking. When will it all be done, Shelley?

SHEL   Not too much longer, don't you worry.

FRAN   Sorry, again, everyone for being out of sorts today. This morning. Well, this afternoon, now. Heavens. I feel woefully unprepared.

ALL sit around the dining table. Awkward silence.

SHELLEY   So, do you have any activities lined up for us today, Francine?

FRAN   Activities? Oh. Well. I actually hadn't thought of any.

GERT   What do you mean you haven't thought of any? You are the queen of overthinking.

FRAN   I guess for once last night I was only living in the moment.

CARL   I don't ever remember you doing that before.

FRAN   There's a first time for everything. (Smiles at HANK)

ALEX   How about while we wait for the food, we all say something we are grateful for, since it's Thanksgiving. Like we always do, Mom, right?

BEN   I am grateful Mom isn't going to try to FedEx me a turkey.

FRAN   I never said I wouldn't.

CARL   Shelley cooks an awesome turkey.

FRAN   It was never her cooking skills in question, Carl.

ALEX   Come on, Ben, what are you most grateful for?

BEN   I dunno. You put me on the spot. What about you?

ALEX   My family obviously.

SHEL   Oh, that's mine too. Family I was born with, as well as the family I chose. You all.

BEN   I'm grateful to Dad for coming all this way to pick me up, since he didn't have to do that. California is going to be awesome.

GERT   I am thankful for Spanx. They do wonders for saggy figures.

BEN   Ew.

GERT   I am just being honest. I look smooth as a stick of butter because of Spanx.

BEN   I repeat. Ew.

CARL   I would be grateful if I didn't have to hear about Gert's undergarments again.

GERT   Your loss.

ALEX   Mom, what are you most grateful for this Thanksgiving?

FRAN   My kids, of course.

BEN   You say that every year.

FRAN   Because it's the truth. All parents feel that way.

BEN   Grandma didn't say that. She said she's grateful for Spanx.

FRAN   Actually, yeah. That's right. Jeesh, Mom.

GERT   Obviously I am grateful for you too.

FRAN   Nice priorities.

GERT   You're a given, though. What thing other than family and kids are you grateful for?

FRAN   I don't know. Um, Hank, you go.

HANK   I'm just grateful to be included. Back to you, Francine.

FRAN   Um... well. I guess...

ALEX   Whatever pops into your head.

FRAN   Uh...

BEN   She isn't going to think of something other than us.

FRAN   Er...

CARL   That's because you kids are part of your Mom's identity.

SHEL   I think it's sweet.

GERT   I think it's a cop out.

FRAN   Would everyone just let me talk?

BEN   We are the best thing that ever happened to her.

ALEX   Full of yourself much?

CARL   Kids, cut it out.

FRAN   (Standing up) I am grateful for red wine! (FRAN has shocked herself) Oh, my gosh. That makes me sound like a lush. But if I'm being honest, red wine last night finally got me to relax, it got me to say some things that were very overdue. Red wine reminded me that I can be fun. That I have a lot I still want to do. That I may soon be alone, but there's no need to sit and mope. There's too many things I have been putting off doing that I want to try. And red wine helped me get a kiss from Hank. And I haven't had a kiss in a while. So... Yeah. Red Wine. Happy Thanksgiving. (She is now thoroughly embarrassed, sits back down)

HANK   I guess I change mine. I am grateful for Francine drinking red wine.

Laughter around the table.

SHEL   Well, that was way more interesting than anything else we said. I think we should all tell a truth now, just like Francine did.

BEN   No, I don't think—

ALEX   That sounds like a bad—

GERT   Oh hell no—

FRAN   Sure, why not. You all got to hear my secret. Red wine makes me say things. In vino veritas is legitimate. So, go on. Tell your truths.

SILENCE.

SHEL   Ok, well, since it was my idea. (Taking a deep breath) Carl, I have something to tell you.

FRAN   Oh dear. Um, maybe this wasn't such a good idea.

CARL   Wh-what?

SHEL   I've known for a little while now. I just think it's time I tell you.

BEN   Oh my God. Am I going to be a big brother?

CARL   You're pregnant?

FRAN   This was a very bad idea.

GERT   Carl, aren't you getting a little old?

CARL   Isn't that the pot calling the kettle black?

SHEL   I'm not pregnant.

CARL   Thank God. Gert's right, I am too old for that.

GERT   Yup.

SHEL   I got into Harvard Law School and come Spring, I am going to be attending as a full time student.

GERT   Unexpected.

FRAN   Oh, wow! Congratulations, Michelle!

CARL   Why did you keep that from me, Shelley? That's great! Well, except. Wait, Harvard as in the Harvard in Boston?

SHEL   That's kind of the only one.

CARL   You're... you're moving to Boston?

SHEL   I have to if I want to pursue law school. I already have an apartment lined up.

CARL   You already have an apartment? In Boston? And you didn't think to consult me about this?

SHEL   I didn't know I would get in when I applied. And then things happened so fast. I didn't know how to tell you.

CARL   "Hey, Carl, honey, I am moving across the country in a few months." That's how you tell me.

SHEL   I was afraid of this happening. You're getting upset.

CARL   You're damn right I'm upset! You're leaving! You're leaving me.

SHEL   I need to follow my dream of being a lawyer, Carl. I've wanted this for a long time.

CARL   I know that. You always said that was your dream. And I support that. But Boston? What does this mean for us, Shelley? I mean, are you breaking up with me? Here? At my ex-wife's house? On fake Thanksgiving?

GERT   This is so awkward.

FRAN   Shush, Mom.

SHEL   I am not breaking up with you, you silly man. I love you.

CARL   Sure sounds like you are breaking up with me.

SHEL   Just because I am going away for school doesn't mean we won't see each other.

BEN   This is so high school. I am living for this drama.

SHEL   Long distance is something we can make work. I just know it.

CARL   Long distance? But... But Shelley. How can I have my fiancée living across the country from me for months on end?

SHEL   Fiancée?

CARL   Well, I wasn't going to do this here, now. But I have a ring for you back home. I was going to propose with roses and champagne when we got back. But now...

SHEL   Oh, Carl! Of course I'll marry you.

CARL   You will?

GERT   Oh hot damn!

SHEL	We can make long distance work.
CARL	Screw it. I could move with you. I could come to Boston. Hell, I'd follow you anywhere. Whatever makes you happy. You bring out the best in me, Shel.
SHEL	Carl, every day you make me feel like I got first place in the Miss Minnesota pageant. (They embrace)
FRAN	What is even happening right now?
ALEX	Oh my gosh, can I be a bridesmaid?
SHEL	Of course. And you too, Francine.
FRAN	I am weirdly so excited right now.
BEN	Sorry, not to put a damper on things. But Dad, I thought I was going to live with you in California. I can't really do that if you are living in Boston.
CARL	We can find you somewhere to live. You can even rent from us.
FRAN	Hang on. Why would Ben need a place to live? He can live on campus.
CARL	You have to go to the college in order to live on campus. (Realizes what he has just said) Shit.
BEN	Dad.
FRAN	What?
ALEX	Uh oh.
GERT	Talk about truths being told.
FRAN	Ben, what is he talking about?
BEN	Look, Mom, I was going to tell you sooner or later...

FRAN	Jesus, Mary, and Joseph.
BEN	I decided I don't want to go to college after all.
FRAN	What?
BEN	I want to go to California to pursue my music and acting career.
FRAN	(Sarcastic) Because the arts get you places in life.
BEN	I need a year off to explore what I really want. And if acting and stuff doesn't pay off, then I can go back and get my degree.
FRAN	I filled out all those damn FAFSA forms for you to just decide you don't want to go to school after all?
BEN	I'm sorry, Mom.
FRAN	If you're not even going to school, why go out to California? Are you trying to get away from me or something?
BEN	Of course not—
FRAN	Oh, never mind. I can't believe you didn't tell me.
BEN	Because I knew you would freak out. Like you are doing right now.
HANK	Maybe you should say five things in the room to ground yourself.
FRAN	I think my anxiety is perfectly founded right about now. You lied to me, Ben.
BEN	I know. I'm sorry. I wish I had told you the truth.
FRAN	No, you wish you hadn't been caught. What next? Mom? You have anything to share with the class? Are

you moving into the nursing home full time in order to have a constant stream of gentlemen callers? Did you contract an STD? Are you going to be a dominatrix for the elderly?

GERT   I am highly offended by those questions.

FRAN   Oh, come on, Mom. Your reputation precedes you. You wear it like a fur coat.

GERT   Do not.

FRAN   You love being the town ho'. You live for it.

GERT   Well, I don't want to be that anymore.

FRAN   Now there's the real shocker.

GERT   No, I mean it, Francie. I am settling down.

FRAN   Yeah, right. You always say you'll settle down when you are dead. Oh, God. You aren't dying are you? Oh, Mom, I am so sorry about saying that thing about being the town ho'.

GERT   Oh, for Pete's sake! No, I'm not dying. But my single life is. I'm in a long term committed relationship. It's Facebook official, which you people would know if you ever accepted my friend request.

FRAN   A... relationship?

GERT   Yes. I am officially off the market. Much to the chagrin of every singleton above the age of sixty-five in this town. I'm done sleeping around.

FRAN   No more... no more nursing home trips?

GERT   No. I'll only be going there to see my... boyfriend. Gosh, even saying it gives me the happy tingles. Unless of course I can convince you to let him move into my room.

FRAN   What?

GERT   Baby steps. I get it.

FRAN   Who is it?

GERT   Well. You might be surprised to know. It's Walter Williams. Hank's dad.

HANK   What?

GERT   I know. But what can I say. The fellow can charm the pants off a nun.

HANK   Oh, no.

GERT   Oh yes. And before you ask, we are using prophylactics.

HANK   I was never going to ask that. But I guess that's good.

FRAN   Mom, don't you think you're a little...

GERT   Old? Were you about to say "old"?

FRAN   No, I wasn't.

GERT   You better not have been. Because for the first time since your father died, Francine, I really feel like a teen again. The clothes, the men, the yoga. Those helped. But it's being able to be myself around Walter that really reminds me what I like most about myself. He doesn't give a rat's ass if I'm dolled up or in sweat suit, if I wear stilettos or chunky white Naturalizer sneakers. He likes that I swear and flirt and goof off. He thinks I am more lively than all the young nurses at the home. And I am not going to try to change myself just because of what society tells me I should do at my age. So for now I'm going to keep dressing how I want, saying what I want, and doing what I want. And for now, all I want to be doing is Walter.

FRAN   Well.

HANK   Hell, I mean, I'm happy for you. But for Pete's sake, please spare me any other details?

GERT   Fair enough.

FRAN   This, this is a lot to handle.

GERT   It's love, Francie. We love who we love.

ALEX   (Quietly) Speaking of which...

FRAN   I just can't handle all of this coming at me.

ALEX   Mom...

SHEL   Francine, I think you need to listen—

FRAN   That feels like all I've been doing, listening to everyone's revelations. It's all too much.

ALEX   But while we are all spilling secrets...

FRAN   I'm sorry, I just can't compute all of this.

ALEX   Mom, listen—

FRAN   Alexis, honey, I just—

ALEX   MOM, I'm gay!

Moment of quiet.

FRAN   What?

ALEX   I like girls, Mom. My date the other day was with a

girl who smelled like Doritos. My type is blondes with accents. Ben knew. Shelley guessed. I was afraid to tell you in case you got upset or it ruined your dreams for me.

FRAN   (Rising from the table, leaving toward the door to upstairs) I'm sorry. I need a minute. (Exits)

Beat of silence.

BEN   (Putting an arm around ALEX) Proud of you, sis. Love you.

ALEX   She just left.

CARL   No matter what, Lex, you are my little girl. Doesn't matter to me who you like.

SHEL   You have us, Sweetpea.

ALEX   She's upset.

CARL   It's a lot to take in.

GERT   She probably left because of me, Alexis.

BEN   Or me.

HANK   Your Mom loves you a lot, Alexis. She told me so. This shouldn't change that. If it does, she's not the good person I thought.

CARL   Maybe we should go for a walk or something.

ALEX   I just didn't think she'd get so upset. I thought...

FRAN   (Offstage) I knew I had it somewhere. I found it! (Enters triumphantly. She is wearing a rainbow shirt, headband, and carrying a massive pride flag, draped like a cape.) Happy Pride, Alexis, my sweet princess lesbian!

FRAN marches over to her daughter. Wraps her in a hug and the flag, and gives her a kiss on the cheek.

ALEX   (Surprised, smiling, relieved, a little close to tears) Mom! Where... how did you find this so fast?

FRAN   I'm sorry, baby girl. I had bought things so we could celebrate Pride with the other holidays, but like Hanukkah I figured you shouldn't celebrate if you're not a part of it. But that was stupid of me. So today will be Pride Thanksgiving.

ALEX   You really freaked me out, Mom. I thought you were mad.

FRAN   Why would I ever be mad? You are and always will be my princess. And what's great is, I won't have to worry about you getting pregnant abroad. Another panic attack averted. I love you, Alexis. Gay or otherwise. Live your truth.

ALEX   Love you too.

BEN   Mom, you seem a little more chilled now. Did you drink more wine?

FRAN   No. I just realized that things change. And it's ok. But don't think I forgot about the whole college thing.

BEN   What about live your truth?

FRAN   Alexis can't help who she likes. You can help your schooling. Here's my condition. You go to California for one year. And if you're not famous by then, you will go to college. Deal?

BEN   Ok, deal.

FRAN   By the way, Shelley, if you need to stay here at all during your breaks from school, my door is always open.

SHEL   Why thank you.

CARL   Does the same go for me?

FRAN   No, you have to call ahead.

Knock at the door, Enter WALTER. He is wearing pajamas. Over which he has a leather jacket. He walks with a cane.

WALT   Gerty, baby! I did it, I escaped!

GERT   Walter! (They embrace)

HANK   Dad? How did you get here? You're supposed to be at the nursing home.

WALT   Hey, Hank. I busted out. Nurse Ratchet nearly had me but I gave her the slip and hopped on my Harley to ride over.

FRAN   He rides a motorcycle?

GERT   It's a Harley brand mobility scooter. It's a two-seater.

WALT   Come on, Gerty. I'll take you on a joy ride. We will be like Bonnie and Clyde, Romeo and Juliet.

ALEX   They all died horrible deaths.

WALT and GERT   Party Pooper.

GERT   Francie, can't I please go? You know what they say. You only live once.

HANK   I need to bring you back, Dad.

WALT   You can't take me alive!

GERT   Francie, can't I keep him in my room?

FRAN   How about we get to know Walter before you start co-habiting. Why don't you stay for dinner, Walter? We are having Pride Thanksgiving.

WALT   What's Pride Thanksgiving?

GERT   Rainbows and turkeys and stuff like that.

WALT   I can dig it, baby. Sounds like the 60s. Good times.

ALEX   Why don't we eat outside at the picnic table. It's rare we get to eat a Thanksgiving outside in New England normally.

FRAN   That's a good idea. Why don't you carry everything out, everyone? I'll bring the turkey out in a few minutes.

CARL, WALT, GERT, ALEX, SHELLEY, BEN, ALL start to exit, carting decorations and food.

GERT   (As she exits, to Alexis) You know. I dated a woman once.

ALEX   Really?

GERT   Yeah. She was great. Maude.

ALEX   Didn't work out, huh?

GERT   No. Not really my type.

BEN   Because she was a woman?

GERT   No. A smoker.

All exit, except HANK and FRANCINE.

HANK   Whirlwind of an afternoon, huh?

FRAN   I can't believe you stuck around for all of that. But somehow you being here made things a little easier.

HANK   I just had to see how it all panned out.

FRAN   I was almost afraid to ask before. Are there any secrets you haven't told me?

HANK   No, I'm a pretty open book.

FRAN   I like that about you. I don't do well with surprises usually.

HANK   I guess the only not-so-secret thing is that I have a thing for you. Surprise.

FRAN   That's a good kind of surprise. (Kisses him)

HANK   That and... I really did like that drag dress. So comfortable.

FRAN   It's all in the craftsmanship. Hank, maybe, once the house is a little emptier, you might want to come over to this side of the house more often.

HANK   I'd like that. And hey, you aren't panicking as much anymore about being here by yourself when the kids go away.

FRAN   You're right. I feel content. In between all my new hobbies, I might even start a new business.

HANK   What's that?

FRAN   Party planning. I don't know if you've noticed, but it's kind of my thing.

HANK   That's kind of perfect for you. Francine's Drag Queens and Party Scenes. (Takes turkey out.)

FRAN   That's perfect! Oh, I have to start planning it out. And I need to make a website. And business cards. I could go to trade shows. What do you think I should charge?

HANK   Oh yeah, you're going to keep plenty busy. You know, alone isn't always a bad thing. It gives you time to sit and reflect on what's good. Now come on, while the food is hot. (HANK exits)

FRAN   (Looking around) Alone isn't always a bad thing. (Sits on a chair, closes her eyes.) Five things, Francine, to keep you grounded. Five things that keep you sane, that you are grateful for this Thanksgiving. (Ticking them off on her fingers) One: Alexis and Ben. Two: Mom. And I guess Walter, since we technically kidnapped him from the nursing home. Three: against all odds, Shelley and Carl. Four: Hank. What a trooper. And Five: Me. I am grateful for me. (Stands up, let's out a contented sigh. Starts for door, grabs a pie on her way out. Turns back around, looks at kitchen once again. Snags a bottle of red wine.) Oh, and I'm grateful for red wine. Me and red wine.

EXIT

THE END

RIGHTS AND PERMISSIONS